The Industrialisation of Arts Education

"In what ways have the demands of industry helped to shape the course of arts education to date, and has industrialisation of the arts been beneficial towards the student experience as we march through the fourth industrial revolution?

Broadhead has curated and contributed this anthology of perspectives, in which academics and practitioners offer important insight into relationships between arts education and the creative industries through discussion of the past, the present and the potential futures.

This book opens a dialogue which could help to define a new concord between arts education and industry for the fifth industrial revolution."
> —Matthew Clark, *Lecturer in Digital Media, Sheffield Hallam University*

"We need a timely reminder that arts education has much to contribute to society and industry - perhaps now more than ever. We need to be able to take notice, to highlight the wider good that can come from arts education while acknowledging its positive social and economic impact. This book brings to light important debates surrounding arts education as it stands in today's society that need to be examined and discussed more widely in order to help shape a better future for arts education and its role for future generations."
> —Alistair Smith, Lecturer, *School of Art and Design, Lincoln College*

"A rigorous yet holistic approach to arts education is needed now more than ever. Young people are leaving school without their creative and critical thinking skills being developed, and often without any sense that this is missing from their lives or that to invest in those skills and ways of thinking can be worthwhile. They miss out, and we miss out; we're poorer for it as human beings and as a society. We need to sit up, be brave, and radically transform our approach to education as a way to be truly transformative. This is an important book as part of that process."
> —Paula Briggs, *CEO and Creative Director of AccessArt, Cambridge*

Samantha Broadhead
Editor

The Industrialisation of Arts Education

Editor
Samantha Broadhead
Leeds Arts University
Leeds, West Yorkshire, UK

ISBN 978-3-031-05016-9   ISBN 978-3-031-05017-6   (eBook)
https://doi.org/10.1007/978-3-031-05017-6

This Palgrave Macmillan imprint is published by the registered company Springer Nature Switzerland AG.
The registered company address is: Gewerbestrasse 11, 6330 Cham, Switzerland

*To the compassionate Paul Whiteley and his furry or feathered friends:
Candy; Felix and Fifi; White Spot; Ivy and Mary; Single and Double;
Amelia and the two Honchos; Little Grey; Limper; Emu and Little Titch.*

FOREWORD

The Creative Industries are an important part of the UK economy and in 2018 it was reported that 1 in 11 jobs was within them (BEIS 2018). Their success is linked to the way that we spend our leisure time, the advancement of technologies and the influence of media streams of communication. The skills needed to be effective as part of the workforce are the skills that our current education system does not promote, because it operates on an outdated curriculum model, which is built around politically driven ideology, leading to a hierarchy of subjects which devalue the arts, despite what consecutive governments say. Creative subjects have been side-lined in favour of the so-called core subjects that emphasise Science, Technology, Engineering and Mathematics (STEM) rather than Science, Technology, Engineering, Arts and Mathematics (STEAM), and the development of a workforce which will be compliant.

Although early years' curriculum models value creativity, children then move into a school system which uses testing from a very early age and which values numeracy and literacy above other subjects, meaning that time for foundation subjects, including the arts, is squeezed out in many schools. Primary schools often teach 'to' the Standard Assessment Tests (SATs) in key stage 2 (the legal term for Years 3, 4, 5 and 6 of schooling maintained in schools in England and Wales). Secondary schools reduce option choices because the UK government and the Office for Standards in Education (OFSTED) are pushing the EBacc (English Baccalaureate) as a measurement of success. Some schools have become exam factories (Coffield & Williamson 2011) and the disappearance of centralised local authority support and being replaced by the academy system has damaged shared-subject specialist pedagogy, quality assurance and the vision and philosophy needed for a contemporary and progressive arts education.

Fewer children study the arts post-14, with subsequent impact on study and career pathways after 16.

Many schools encourage the knowledge-rich curriculum which does not emphasise how knowledge is used, but it is about rote learning of factual information. The Department for Education (England) cherry picks the research that it wants to use for curriculum models. The government also measures the value of degrees by the amount of money that a graduate earns a few years into their career, taking no account that many of those in the arts are self-employed or freelancers, and does not measure job satisfaction or the value to oneself of doing what you love to do. It now even refers to some higher education courses as 'low value'. The value, of course, being purely fiscal.

What happens in schools has a domino effect on the number of people studying creative subjects in further and higher education. Ultimately the talent pool is narrowing and this will have an impact on the cultural sector, where there currently is a lack of diversity in its workforce. The danger is that only those who can afford an arts education will be able to access highly skilled careers in the Creative Industries. This book argues for the importance of arts education at all levels for the future growth and flourishing of the sector.

To be successful and world-leading the Creative Industries need young people and adults to become creative, articulate, problem-solvers and innovators who can think critically and collaborate. Our current education system with its misplaced values is not creating the diverse thinkers and innovators that will be needed to help the Creative Industries thrive in the post-pandemic world. The current government has deliberately sought to silence creative thinking and actions through a toxic 'one-solution-fits-all' pedagogy.

This book looks at the various relationships arts education and its students have with the industry and how those relationships are influenced by various neoliberal policies. It also explores how educators have to reconcile their professional values about what constitutes a good education with the various demands on their curricula, including the need to prepare their students in an ethical way for creative careers.

Coffield, F. & Williamson, B. (2011). *From exam factories to communities of discovery: The democratic route*. London: Institute of Education, University of London.

Department for Business, Energy and Industrial Strategy (BEIS). (2018). Industrial strategy: Creative industries sector deal. https://assets. publishing.service.gov.uk/government/uploads/system/uploads/ attachment_data/file/695097/creative-industries-sector-deal-print.pdf Accessed 08 March 2022.

Visiting Professor for Education Through Art   Susan Coles
University of Sunderland
Sunderland, UK
Secretary to the All-Party
Parliamentary Group on Art, Craft,
Design in Education, London, UK

PREFACE

The origins of this book began with a symposium, 'Aspiration and Constraint in the Post-COVID Post-Compulsory Crisis', on 5 October 2020 organised by the British Educational Research Association (BERA) Special Interest Group for Post-Compulsory and Lifelong Learning. This event opened up conversations between researchers interested in workplace learning, vocational and higher education and arts educators.

The ensuing dialogue led to a collaborative symposium between the University of Derby and Leeds Arts University, 'The Industrialisation of Arts Education', held 16 March 2021. The multi-discipline programme included perspectives from specialists in animation, creative writing, fashion branding, music, education and employment. The contributors came from research, practitioner and educational backgrounds and their work is underpinned by close-to-practice research and scholarship that interrogates the policies and practices related to arts education and the creative industries. The debates have now been developed as part of this publication.

It seems that within the context of UK higher education the language and practices of the arts have been industrialised. Within the cultural or creative industries artists, designers and makers are described as producers. Furthermore, due to research assessment, such as the Research Excellent Framework, paintings, drawings, exhibitions, musical performances, film and designs are perceived as outputs.

Each chapter of this book brings with it a particular orientation of industry to arts education, such as teaching and learning for industry, the impact of industry-focused policies and industrialised systemic influences.

The extent to which arts pedagogies have been informed by the agendas of the cultural industries as well as wider neoliberal ideologies is considered. This leads to fundamental questions about, firstly, the many, contradictory functions of arts education and, secondly, the ways teaching and learning practices have evolved.

This book would be of interest to students, researchers and academics who are interested in arts further and higher education as well as post-16 technical and vocational education.

ACKNOWLEDGEMENTS

I would like to take this opportunity to thank Christopher Graham, Dr Jill Fernie-Clarke, Henry Gonnet, Frances Norton, Kate O'Donnell and Leeds Arts University for the support they have given me and the chapter authors in writing this book.

Leeds, West Yorkshire, UK   Samantha Broadhead

Contents

NOTES ON CONTRIBUTORS

Samantha Broadhead is Head of Research at Leeds Arts University, North of England, and researches mature students' experiences in art and design education. She serves on the editorial board of the *Journal of Widening Participation and Lifelong Learning* and carries out review work for FACE (Forum for Access and Continuing Education). Broadhead's work on access and widening participation is published. Broadhead has co-authored with Professor Maggie Gregson *Practical Wisdom and Democratic Education: Phronesis, Art and Non-traditional Students* (Macmillan Palgrave, 2018). She also has co-authored with Rosemarie Davies and Anthony Hudson *Perspectives on Access to Higher Education: Practice and Research* (2019).

Bill Esmond is Associate Professor of Education and Employment and co-convener for the British Educational Research Association (BERA) post-compulsory and lifelong learning special interest group. His research interests are related to vocational education and training. His upcoming book with Liz Atkins is *Educating for the Hour-glass Economy: Technical Elites, Reproduction and Social Justice* (Routledge).

Jason Huxtable is an educator and performer, active within higher education (HE) for over 15 years and across genres. Performance experience has ranged from major Pop/Rock festivals (Glastonbury), Jazz (Cheltenham) and Classical (Los Angeles Philharmonic). As an HE practitioner, he is interested in the process of student transformation through application of tenets of critical pedagogy within music curricular. Huxtable is an Honorary Member of the Royal Birmingham Conservatoire (HonRBC) for success in the music industry.

Michael Smith has a well-established teaching practice; he is interested in storytelling and creative problem-solving through animation. His research activities focus on understanding the impact industry has on higher education and animation pedagogical practices.

Eleanor Snare is a senior lecturer at Leeds Arts University, UK, with an MA in Social History of Art and a BA in Design and Applied Arts.

Karen Tobias-Green is a course leader and Lecturer in Creative Writing and Research Methods. She is a published fiction writer and poet and has recently completed her DPhil in Education.

ABBREVIATIONS

A-Level	Advanced-Level Qualifications
BA	Bachelor of Arts
BFI	The British Film Institute
BIS	The Department for Business Innovation and Skills
BTEC	Business and Technology Education Council Qualifications
CIC	The Creative Industries Council
CMA	Competitions and Markets Authority
CNAA	The Council for National Academic Awards
DATEC	The Design and Art Technical Education Council
Des. R.A.C.	Diploma in Design from the Royal Art College
DfE	Department for Education
DipAD	Diploma in Art and Design
DNA	Deoxyribonucleic Acid
EBacc	English Baccalaureate
EU	The European Union
GCSE	General Certificate of Secondary Education
HE	Higher Education
HEFCE	The Higher Education Funding Council for England
HEIs	Higher Education Institutions
HMRC	Her Majesty's Revenues and Customs
IABC	Industrial Arts Bursaries Competitions
iCeGS	The International Centre for Guidance Studies
IES	The Institute of Environmental Sciences
IfATE	The Institute for Apprenticeships and Technical Education
IGS	The Industrial Growth Society

IR4	The Fourth Industrial Revolution
ISM	The Incorporated Society of Musicians
LAU	Leeds Arts University
LED	Light-Emitting Diode
LEO	Longitudinal Education Outcomes
Ltd	Limited Company
NCDAD	The National Council for Diplomas in Arts and Design
NDD	The National Diploma in Design
OECD	The Organisation for Economic Co-operation and Development
OfS	Office for Students
POLAR	The Participation of Local Areas
QAA	The Quality Assurance Agency for Higher Education
RAF	Royal Air Force
RSA	Royal Society of the Arts
SDGs	The Sustainable Development Goals
STEM	Science, Technology, Engineering and Mathematics
T-Level	Technical-Based Qualifications
TEF	Teaching Excellence Framework
TV	Television
UAL	University of the Arts London
VET	Vocational Education and Training
VFX	Visual Effects

LIST OF FIGURES

Introduction

Samantha Broadhead

Abstract The introduction begins with a brief history of public arts education in relation to industry in order to establish that arts education has always had a complex relationship with industrialists and manufacturing businesses. Commentators during the nineteenth and twentieth centuries have suggested that arts education and industry should work together to improve the quality of manufactured goods. For example, the Bauhaus in Germany embraced industrial processes as part of its teaching when students were encouraged to design prototypes for products with a 'machine aesthetic' that could be manufactured on a large scale. During the postwar years there was a growth in leisure and entertainment activities such as film and television along with other white-collar occupations such as advertising and graphic design that signalled the growth of the creative industries. The range of courses available to prospective students widened to include these emerging cultural practices.

The text then continues to discuss how arts education has been informed by the agendas of the manufacturing sector and the cultural industries over time as well as the current impact of neoliberal ideologies.

S. Broadhead (✉)
Leeds Arts University, Leeds, UK
e-mail: sam.broadhead@leeds-art.ac.uk

This leads to fundamental questions about the contradictory relationships between arts education and industry. The introduction then goes on to summarise the chapters that consider the tensions that exist when educating students for industry, the influence of rationality, standardisation and instrumentalism on educational policies and the impact of industrialisation on arts pedagogies.

Keywords Art • Higher education • Industry • Creative industries • Neoliberalism

ARTS EDUCATION: WHAT DOES IT COMPRISE?

Defining the arts can be challenging as new art practices are often being created where new forms are tested and stretched, breaking previously established disciplinary boundaries (Adajian, 2018). The particular arts subjects addressed in this book include animation, jewellery making, creative writing, fashion branding and popular music. Many of these disciplines would not have existed as courses until well after the post-war expansion of the creative industries (Banks, 2017). But much of the content of this book alludes to wider activities that relate to creativity, innovation and imagination (Finn & Fancourt, 2018). There are a multitude of related activities that are too numerous to mention but include; drawing, sculpting, painting, designing, sewing, photographing, composing, performing, editing, filming and making.

Arts education has historically and currently utilised a myriad of methods and approaches to teaching and learning. Shreeve (2011), Orr and Shreeve (2017) have described the pedagogies of uncertainty that are often used in studios and arts learning contexts to facilitate creative practice. Broadhead (2015) drawing upon the work of Bernstein has identified the invisible pedagogies of studio practice where arts learning is conceived as being open ended, experimental and student-centred (Bernstein, 1997, 2003). Much earlier forms of arts education have been more formal and prescriptive where students learned to draw from plaster casts of idealised forms and through life drawing (the human figure) (Miller, 2003). Older methods of arts education sometimes continue in conjunction with more contemporary approaches within art schools, colleges and universities.

The arts and crafts have also been taught outside formal institutions through the atelier system, where students or apprentices learn directly from the craftsperson or artist in their workshop (Warren, 1916).

Education in other kinds of arts institutions such as music conservatoires comprise different approaches to pedagogy and have different histories (Blackstone, 2019; Duffy, 2013).

How does arts education then relate to the notion of industrialisation? Read (1961) was distressed that many people thought that the arts and industry were mutually exclusive in the mid-twentieth century, arguing that art schools needed to embrace industry and the new technologies associated with it. However, historically there has been a long and complicated relationship between arts education and industry. There are at least three possible orientations of arts education in relation to the industrial context.

Firstly, there is the notion of educating students to meet the needs of industry. Secondly, there is the influence the various forms of industrialisation have had on arts educational philosophy and art practices. Thirdly how industrial processes such as the division of labour, mechanisation, rationalism and instrumentalism have influenced educational policies and institutional structures that in turn have had an impact on arts education. At the same time, it is acknowledged that there have been other positions that have taken a critical view on industrialisation that have also had an impact on arts education such as the nineteenth-century arts and crafts movement led by William and May Morris and the responsible design movement of the mid- to late twentieth century (Pevsner, 1964; Whiteley, 1993).

The introduction is organised according to the four industrial revolutions where the consensus is that the first one started in the late 1700s, the second in the late 1800s, the third in the mid-1940s and currently we are in the fourth industrial revolution. The relation arts education had to industry during these historical periods is briefly discussed. This establishes that arts education has had a long-standing relationship with industry, although that relationship has been complex and contested. The focus has been on the plastic arts in art, craft and design schools as they initially appeared to have the most explicit and instrumental function as designers and makers for industry. However, arts schools during their histories did and do also teach other creative subjects such as photography, film-making, performing arts and creative writing. Within this book an expanded understanding of how a wide range of artistic practices in education have been impacted by industrialisation is explored.

PUBLIC ARTS EDUCATION FOR INDUSTRY: A BRIEF HISTORY

Pre-industrial arts education for practicing artists was mostly based on an apprenticeship system. This was where a 'master' would train apprentices within their studio. This can be inferred from Giorgio Vasari's descriptions of artists' training such as that of Michelangelo, in his book, *Lives of the Most Excellent Painters, Sculptors, and Architects* originally written in 1550 (1998 edition). Often the skills of the father would be passed on to the son producing generations of male artists (Pevsner, 1940). During the eighteenth century formal arts education professionalised artists through the 1768 founding of the Royal Academy in Great Britain (Denvir, 1983). Genteel young ladies, excluded from the Royal Academy, were taught embroidery, sketching and water colour painting by private tutors to enhance their accomplishments desirable for good marriages (Parker & Pollock 1981; Parker, 1984; Nochlin, 1989).

The late eighteenth century is cited as being when the first industrial revolution brought with it dramatic technological, socio-economic and cultural changes that brought new forms of transport, modes of information transfer, urbanisation and industrialised modes of production (Skilton & Hovsepian, 2018). Romans (2005) pointed out that this change decreased the number of trained artisans as large parts of the population began working in factories. A call for publicly funded arts education came from the Select Committee on Arts and Manufactures (1835–1836) where it was recognised that there was a need to educate artisans, the industrial classes and the consumers of the new goods being produced (Cooksey, 2006; Romans, 2005). The need for designs to be communicated to manufactures through drawing was seen to be very important in improving the quality of manufactured goods. As a result, a school of design was opened in London in 1837 that quickly supported 21 'Branch' schools in the industrial regions (Cooksey, 2006; Romans, 2005). The belief that a training in art and design would ultimately improve the quality of manufactured products underpinned the initial growth of art schools and this idea continued throughout the nineteenth and twentieth centuries.

Henry Cole attained the post of General Superintendent of the newly titled Department of Practical Art in 1852 and Richard Redgrave held the position of Art Superintendent. Cole introduced a uniform curriculum guided by annually published rules and regulations that rationalised the delivery and purpose of state-funded arts education (Cooksey, 2006).

There was a tension between the idea that art schools provided training for local industry and Cole's centralised, regimented and inflexible curriculum, the National Course of Instruction, even though it did embed design in its content. This approach to art, the South Kensington style of teaching that promoted the flattening of natural forms based on geometric convention, spread to the United States. Walter Smith (a graduate of South Kensington National Art Training School and former art master in charge of the branch school at Leeds) was appointed to the School of the Art Institute of Chicago to provide drawing curricula for industry, "by exploiting popular and patriotic belief in drawing's less tangible qualities: that its practice cultivated habits of neatness and accuracy, taste, imagination, and the powers of invention" (Jaffee, 2005, p. 43). This benefited the local print industry that called for trained designers with drawing skills.

Cole also promoted principles of 'taste' through the creation of a Museum of Manufactures which was sited in Marlborough House in London in 1857. The Museum drew upon objects acquired from the Great Exhibition, 1851, as well as plaster casts, previously used as teaching resources in the previous schools of design. This collection led to the later establishment of the Victoria and Albert Museum in Exhibition Road, London (Cooksey, 2006; Jaffee, 2005).

Arts education was seen to be important for industrialists, but it was also seen as important for the public to have an informed taste, which would encourage them to appreciate goods of quality and so create an appetite for good design. The notion of taste encapsulated not only aesthetic awareness but also moral improvement (Romans, 2005). The criticism that industrialists and manufacturing workshop managers had poor taste and discernment (Pevsner, 1937; Pevsner, 1964) has been one that reoccurs through the next century and employed to justify the importance of art and design education. The curricula delivered in art schools were divided into fine arts and applied arts that comprised drawing, design for industry and handicrafts.

Questions about the role of the fine arts (painting and sculpture) in applied arts education were not always resolved. Also, how a training in handicrafts could be transposed into an industrial context was not completely apparent.

CRITICISM OF MANUFACTURED GOODS CONTINUES

A dissatisfaction with the quality of British manufacturing continued through into the twentieth century and after the First World War there was an appetite to make changes. Gordon Forsyth, a ceramic designer, teacher, writer and a leading advocate for industrial pottery design (Palmer and Dobson, 1995), wrote to the editor of the Staffordshire Sentinel, "enemy countries were making giant strides in competitive markets through the very same characteristics that we were blindly refusing to accept" (Forsyth, 1918, p. 3). He was critical of industrialists that did not invest in design education throughout the war years.

Eatwell (1989) claimed Forsyth's contribution was the creative crafts-manship model which was compatible with industry. At Burslem School of Art he advocated the use of hand painting. His approach gained more traction when Forsyth was appointed Art Advisor to the British Manufacturers Federation in 1921. There were critics of the promotion of hand painting as seen from the observations made by the chair of the Ceramic Society at a meeting held in 1925;

> Mr Forsyth praised the return to almost entire hand-decoration. Was that not going too far back in the attempt to produce fine art? It must not be overlooked that nowadays we are living in an age of machinery, ought we not therefore make the very best of machinery? (Spours, 1988, p. 65)

The role the handicrafts played in arts education and the relevance to industries underpins this comment. Also, Forsyth's ideas were derived in his own industry experience but were they also greatly informed by Victorian art and design pedagogies and production methods? There was a sense that 'art' as an ornament could be applied to the surface of manu-factured goods. For example, Clarice Cliff (a once part-time student of Burslem School of Art) was able to make flawed old-fashioned table ware saleable by painting modern patterns on them (Spours, 1988). Also, man-ufacturing processes that still relied on human production lines such as ceramics, jewellery and watch-making required workers with making and handicraft skills. Industrialisation in these manufacturing areas was through the division of labour rather than the use of mechanised production.

Forsyth was attuned to the needs of the ceramic industry believing that ideal teachers were those from local communities who understood the students and the regional industries better. Also, effective education was through live briefs that were based on the actual industrial work the students would be undertaking. Forsyth considered that the ideal art school was where craftspeople learn a trade while developing an inner self. Sykes (2008) noted that the 1946 report Art Education published by the Ministry of Education praised the approach to training in the Midlands as being most compatible with industry and advocated executed design as a national pedagogic model.

However, other commentators continued to be critical of the lack of quality of British goods that was seen to spring from a lack of artistic knowledge, appreciation and skill. Nikolaus Pevsner in his 1937 Enquiry into industrial art in England noted that the pottery industry had not utilised the skills of a designer. This led to inferior standards and the reoccurrence of traditional patterns. He wrote:

> These imitations are due to staff managers or so-called staff managers. The employment of full-time designers is less a matter of course in the pottery industry than the public might expect. 90% of Stoke firms have no designer, sales experience is regarded as more important than a grasp of design, so far as design is concerned his work consists of the buying of lithographs for transfer, adapting the imitations of new ones from next door. (Pevsner, 1937, p. 78)

These comments echo those being made 100 years previously that drove the first publicly funded art schools. Read (1961) reflected that industrialists were indifferent to aesthetic values, because they responded to public taste. He asked, "does the public need education in good taste so that industrialists will then supply the goods the public discerns as good design?" Art education was important for both consumers and producers of goods. Some leaders of British manufacturing still continued to have a limited or superficial understanding of what good design could be and how it could improve their wares and make firms more competitive, relying instead on styles, materials and processes that were familiar and conservative. Read saw the problem as educational where design was presented as a cultural veneer from previous ages when processes of production were different. Read was very critical of art schools that retained a mode of teaching that was based on drawing from the antique plaster casts. He proposed that there needed to be a new consciousness of aesthetic form and a revision of the educational system.

Machine Aesthetic

The second industrial revolution got under way during the latter part of the nineteenth century. Industrial processes, transport, public lighting and modes of communication were electrified. Also, modes of production were rationalised creating assembly lines (Jerath, 2021; Skilton & Hovsepian, 2018). Fordist modes of production became prevalent along with Taylorism and the scientific management of labour (Watson, 2019). These indicators of modernity informed modernist art and design movements such as Russian Constructivism beginning in 1914 and Dutch De Stijl (1917–1931).

Read (1961) when reflecting on art and industry in the UK was influenced by the ideas springing from the Bauhaus (1919–1933) in Weimar and Dessau under the leadership of Walter Gropius. There was a clear vision of the relationship between the visual arts, handicrafts, education and industry.

> Art is regarded as something distinct from the process of machine production, something which must be taught as a distinct (though 'basic) subject, afterward to be introduced into the processes of industry. But obviously, the factory itself must be the school of design, or the school of design must become in some real sense a factory. (Read, 1961, p. 116)

Gropius articulated a model derived from the Bauhaus where the art school was not exactly a factory, but a laboratory where through materials and process experimentation students could find new forms that considered function, rationality and standardisation (Gropius, 1965). The aim of the Bauhaus was to produce prototypes that could be manufactured (Gropius 1925 in Heskett, 1984). All students would be taught basic visual language together and then later would specialise. These ideas travelled to Chicago through the teachings of Moholy Nagy, who was leader of the Bauhaus' preliminary course (Jaffee, 2005). Leeds College of Art also designed its basic design course along these lines (Miller, 2003).

Gropius reflected that,

> The Bauhaus accepted the machine as the essentially modern vehicle of form, and sought to come to terms with it. Its workshops were really laboratories in which practical designs for present-day goods were conscientiously worked out as models for mass production, and were continually being improved on. (Gropius, 1965, p. 53)

When students were making objects by hand they had at the same time to be fully cognizant of mass-production techniques. The aim of experimentation in the laboratory was to make prototypes that could be put into production. Design was no longer conceived of something that was applied to the surface of products, but integral to the evolution of form through the exploration of materials appropriate to machine production.

> The constructors of these models had also to be fully acquainted with factory methods of mechanical mass-production, which are radically different from those of handicraft, although the various parts of the prototypes they evolved had naturally to be made by hand. It is from the individual peculiarities of every type of machine that the new, but still individual 'genuineness' and 'beauty' of its products are derived; whereas illogical machine imitation of hand-made goods infallibly bears the stamp of a make-shift substitute. (Gropius, 1965, p. 53)

The machine aesthetic led to forms that looked as if they were manufactured rather than hand crafted, even though the prototypes were produced by individuals who were experimenting with materials in studios or laboratories (Gropius 1925 in Heskett, 1984). The industrialisation of art education in this case was not teaching students to apply a veneer of historical style to the surface of an object to suggest it was a quality item. It was about fully embracing the production technology and designing curricula that encouraged students to think about how their designs could be mass produced. This led to iconic designs such as the Marcel Breuer 1928 B33 cantilever chair and Marianne Brandt's 1924 teapot. Forms were abstracted and had clean lines, sleek surfaces and a holistic sense of overall design rather than detailed surface ornamentation.

The machine aesthetic did not only impact on the visual arts. Oskar Schlemmer's Triadisches Ballett performed when he was at the Bauhaus from 1921 to 1929, the ballet toured, helping to spread the Bauhaus philosophy. In the 1920s Arnold Schönberg's 12-tone method was created at the same time that Kandinsky was working in a strictly formalistic Bauhaus style. Schönberg in 1923 took over the direction of the music school in Weimar, in order to be closer to the Bauhaus movement.

The Bauhaus also had a clear understanding of the function of educating fine artists in relation to industry. Both Gropius (1965) and Read (1961) understood artists as being like mathematicians, working with abstract form—pushing the boundaries of aesthetic possibilities through research and experimentation. This creative practice would eventually inform the design for the machine age.

GROWTH OF THE CREATIVE INDUSTRIES

After the Second World War there was a boom in automation, electronics and mass-communication. The use of computers was slowly gaining traction. This growth has been described as the third industrial revolution (Skilton & Hovsepian, 2018). It is also during that time that the creative industries start to flourish. Mark Banks (2017) noted that in the UK and other economically developed nations there was growth in radio, television, newspaper and magazine publishing, advertising, the music industry and wider creative arts during the mid-twentieth century. He went on to say, "As part of the wider growth in post-industrial, service and tertiary sector jobs, the expanding territories of culture, arts, entertainment and 'mass-communications' were assumed to be opening up to everyone, in an unprecedented way" (p. 91). This could be seen as part of a more general expansion in white-collar, service and entertainment industries catering for those with increased leisure time.

> [The] mid-twentieth century saw widest spectrum of people become involved in the cultural industries as consumers, workers and producers... the cultural industries not only radically advanced the provision of public art and mass creativity but created a whole new world of cultural manufacture, employment and trade. (Banks, 2017, p. 90)

Post-war advances in welfare, education, health and social care influenced creative aspirations of working- and middle-class people. Forms of commercial popular culture exploded due to technical innovations that led to less expensive printing, new forms of art making, film-making, musical performance and recording. Public funding for 'uncommercial' art was deemed to provide society with civility and aesthetic elevation.

Marglin and Schor (1990) described the 'long boom' as a golden age of capitalism that lasted from 1945 until the early 1970s. Towards the end of this time span, there were changes taking place in art schools that appeared to respond to the increase of cultural industry white-collar jobs. At the end of 1970, the National Council for Diplomas in Art and Design (NCDAD) also known as the Summerson Committee and National Advisory Council on Art Education chaired by Sir William Coldstream issued a report to clarify the whole post-16 art and design education system. The report described two routes through art education. It was recommended that, most students should do A-Levels, foundation and then a three year HE course.

Group A would do a Foundation (specialise) and a three-year course (BA)

Group B would enter art school at 16 four-year course that would be more vocational. (Miller, 2003, p. 81)

There was a suggestion that the study of fine art was not necessarily central to all studies in the design field. This was a change in philosophy from that of Walter Gropius who believed that all art and design students should initially be taught visual analysis together before specialising in a particular discipline. By 1973 the NCDAD became the Board of Studies for Art and Design within the Council for National Academic Awards (CNAA) and worked towards turning the DipAD into BA (Hons). By situating art and design within the context of higher education there was an acknowledgement of the academic aspects of art education, including critical and contextual studies along with high-level problem-solving, discernment and technical skill. Graduates would be qualified for white-collar jobs in the cultural and design industries.

In the 1980s the vocational 4 years for 16-year olds was transformed into the Business and Technology Education Council (BTEC) comprising a 2-year National Diploma and a 2-year Higher National Diploma in specialist vocational courses such as graphic design or fashion; students could then go onto higher education or a technician job in the design industry (Miller, 2003).

The changes in accreditation through vocational and higher educational routes that occurred during the 1970s and 1980s reflected a stratification within creative industries. This was between those who were trained to be technicians and those who would become creative leaders and it is likely that this division was along social class and gender lines (Banks, 2010; Duberley et al., 2017; Hughes, 2012). Banks (2017) has argued that the creative industries continue to perpetuate inequalities in working conditions and recognition in relation to gender, social class, race and disability.

SOCIALLY RESPONSIBLE DESIGN

During the third industrial revolution designers were beginning to question the ethics of the modernist approach that made industry a central focus of the design process. There were also concerns that designers were working uncritically for a consumer culture that was unsustainable and unethical:

> Like the US and Japan [Britain] enthusiastically pursued an uncritical free market system and abandoned its broader responsibilities. When designers do likewise, operating solely as a tool of consumerism, their status becomes questionable. (Wood, 1990, p. 9)

Whiteley (1993) identified the 'green' design movement as a radical critique of consumerist design while at the same time acknowledging the rise of the 'green consumer'. By buying products from places such as The Body Shop shoppers are registering their commitment to 'planet-friendly' products. However, the danger is that some manufacturers apply only a surface of greenness to their products, in the similar way earlier designers applied a veneer of historical style (Whiteley, 1993).

An important text was written by Victor Papanek, Design for the Real World. It was very critical of consumer-led design and called for a socially responsible practice:

> In an age of mass production when everything must be planned and designed, design has become the most powerful tool with which man shapes his tools and environments (and, by extension, society and himself). This demands high social and moral responsibility from the designer. (Papanek, 1974, p. 9)

It could be argued that an art and design education that was situated in higher education could potentially develop a politically aware, socially responsible and ethically orientated designer. A curriculum based on teaching design skills could also provide a context for critical thinking around the power of design to impact on the world.

Although Papanek's gendered language partly detracts from some of his sentiments, his work opens up the discourse around the relationship of design and sustainable practice. Whiteley (1993) acknowledges the work of The Feminist Design Collective, founded in 1978 in addressing some of the patriarchal assumptions perpetuated through design practice and education.

Neoliberalism, Employability, Sustainability and Widening Participation in the Twenty-First Century

Commentators consider that we are now in the fourth industrial revolution. Digital technologies, robotics, virtual reality, artificial intelligence and increased connectivity have had a huge impact on people's lives and work patterns (Makridakis, 2017; Skilton & Hovsepian, 2018). It has also influenced, along with the more recent COVID-19 pandemic, the ways in which people consume culture (Bakhshi, 2020). Baker (2016) has suggested that previously technical revolutions had created jobs but that the fourth (digital) industrial revolution will not follow this pattern. He argues that education needs to focus on active learning, technical entrepreneurial skills and personal and collaborative skills for living and working harmoniously with others.

The relationship between arts education and industry has always been complex. However, any vision of how this relationship could flourish in the early twenty-first century remains unclear as we (the contributors to this book) are currently still living within the fourth industrial revolution.

Currently, any model of art and design teaching and learning that relates to the needs of the creative industries and manufacturing also needs to operate in a highly regulated educational landscape. Policies regarding issues such as employability, sustainability and widening participation mediate the ways in which arts education is designed, delivered, evaluated and valued. These educational policies and practices operate in a wider paradigm of neoliberalism (Bhopal & Shain, 2018; Tett & Hamilton, 2021).

Bhopal and Shain (2018) have identified the tensions between social justice and educational systems that are dominated by market-led reforms. They noted that educational discourse, policy and practice have become dominated by competition, benchmarking and target-driven accountability.

Students including those who study creative subjects have become increasingly responsible for funding their education and are positioned by institutions as customers who have a choice in their 'educational product' (Williams, 2013). To help students and parents identify quality educational provision, institutions are measured using data from experience surveys, participation, retention and achievement statistics and graduate outcomes along with other indicators so they can be ranked (Atherton, 2018).

Burke (2002) pointed out that although the neoliberal and instrumental context of higher education promotes access and widening participation, this is driven by possible economic benefits for individuals, communities and for nation states. Da Costa (2022) argued that a pervasive neoliberalism driving educational policy would create a hostile global climate for those pursuing the creative arts and wider participation in higher education.

Rogoff (2006) also critiqued the bureaucracy and outcome-orientated higher education as being in discordance with art school pedagogy:

> Odd, then that such an unstable pedagogy should have been captured and held hostage by such an overwhelming bureaucracy—unless perhaps the bureaucracy is afraid of the very challenge such an approach would represent to its sovereignty. (Rogoff, 2006, p. 7)

The suggestion was that arts-based pedagogies spring from a different paradigm than the systemic policy and institutional context in which it operates and this will inevitably lead to tensions.

At the same time, Bichard recognised that, "The creative industries are becoming ever more significant in the UK, and represent a larger proportion of the economy than anywhere else in the world" (Bichard in Sykes, 2008, p. 56). Arts educators were encouraged to collaborate or partner with industry, as it was suggested that employers were involved with "work-based modules, provision of work experience placements, and assessment of student performance" (HEFCE, 2000, p. 8). The current UK Quality Assurance Agency for Higher Education (QAA) benchmark statements for art and design encourage some of this activity, stating:

> Knowledge and understanding of commercial and professional practice is developed in a variety of ways. Externally-set, 'live' projects, placements and internships are a common feature of many courses. (QAA, 2019, p. 11)

There is a drive that students should be employable after they have completed their studies and it is suggested that engagement with appropriate industrial and business contexts can contribute to this. The link between employers and education is even more explicit in the UK's relatively new T-Level programmes that support vocational and technical routes into industry (DfE, 2020).

Ideas relating to responsible green design continue to have relevance and higher education is seen to play a significant role in attaining the Sustainable Development Goals (SDGs) (Ferguson & Roofe, 2020; Alm et al., 2021). But how does the imperative to educate for ecologically responsible designers sit with the need to engage with industries that do not necessarily have this ethical perspective?

Finally, access and widening participation is an important aspect of educational regulation. For example, higher education institutions are required to address gaps in participation, retention and attainment between different social groups in their access and participation plans (OfS, 2021). However, some of the creative industries that arts students may be going into are highly stratified according to gender, race, class and disability (Banks, 2017; Burger & Easton, 2020). How are students prepared for employment in contexts where they might have unequal working conditions and opportunities for promotion?

Summary of Chapters

In the proceeding chapters, six researchers and practitioners reflect on the industry-arts education relationship. Three themes can be identified in their work: the tensions recognised by subject specialists educating for industry; the contradictions between educating for employability and also for sustainability and finally the monitoring of arts teaching through quality assurance measures.

Chapter 2 by Esmond argues that the place of all subjects in mainstream curricula (in all sectors) is increasingly defined by their perceived contribution to student employability, economic growth and the competitiveness of nations. Policy discourses that frame educational practice in terms of the 'value' of disciplines, supported by measures such as the Longitudinal Education Outcomes (LEO) data, validate additional funding for science, technology, engineering and mathematics (STEM) and threaten 'low-returns' courses (such as art and music). In post-16 education, subjects unable to conform to the norms of industry placements are likely to find themselves further marginalised. This diminution of creative areas reflects wider societal requirements for the arts to justify any requests for support in terms of their contribution to the national economy rather than to human flourishing. Esmond critically evaluates the implementation of T-Levels; these are an alternative to apprenticeships and other 16–19 courses. Equivalent to three A-levels, a T-Level focuses on the vocational skills that aim to help students gain skilled employment. Esmond's analysis reveals that the creative arts are not well-served by these qualifications and that they have been designed in such a way that does not reflect how the creative industries operate.

Tobias-Green in Chap. 3 approaches the topic of the industrialisation of arts education from a perspective informed by creative writing. Beginning with a reflection on the various definitions of industrialisation and art education, Tobias-Green explores some of the ways in which arts education has been mechanised and technologised. It offers some provocations, examples, questions, experiences and possible responses to the issues thrown up by these phenomena. By positioning arts writing at the centre of the storm Tobias-Green asks the reader to consider their own experiences of art, writing and the self through the lens of the tricky and layered phrase *The Industrialisation of Art Education*.

Broadhead in Chap. 4 discusses the case of Ann O'Donnell, a jewellery designer-maker who was educated at Leeds and London art schools during the 1950s. Working in industry was a requirement of her jewellery and silversmithing course. O'Donnell's experiences during her work placement at Charles Horner Ltd were analysed in order to discover how effective the approach of 'preparing designers for industry' was in practice. O'Donnell's story revealed a friction between her creative education and the jewellery manufacturing setting. After graduating from the Royal College of Art in the late 1950s O'Donnell taught the jewellers in her locality of Leeds. It is argued she created curricula that were responsive to the needs of the local industries, whose workers needed training in skills. She also supported her students to become creative and imaginative while giving opportunities to those who could not access full-time education.

Smith in Chap. 5 draws upon his many years' experience leading an undergraduate animation course to highlight the tensions between the needs of industry and the purpose of arts higher education. Some of the issues raised by Smith are similar to those explored by Broadhead, but from a twenty-first-century perspective.

Smith argues that industry leaders call for animation higher education to produce graduates who are highly skilled, technically adept and are 'ready for industry'. He asks if this places an unrealistic pressure on students—that they should be technically excellent upon completion of their undergraduate studies?

Smith identifies the root of the issue as a need to appreciate that training and education are different. For Smith, training involves teaching the individual to become competent in carrying out specific tasks or sets of processes. He proposes that education, on the other hand, is a journey, an exploration of a subject, developing a deep understanding of a practice or area of specialist study. Training can be part of education but not the whole. The emphasis that industry representatives place on purely technical skills presents issues for educators who are trying to enable students to become independent thinkers who can function creatively within their chosen discipline to a high level.

Snare in Chap. 6 has a background in fashion branding higher education and has also worked in industry. By drawing upon a reflective teaching diary that she kept for a year, an interrogation of pedagogic emotional dilemmas is undertaken. Snare considers the contradictions that are faced by educators on a daily basis where they attempt to reconcile the need to prepare students for working within a fashion industrial context with the evidence that such industries are unsustainable and damaging to the Earth. Indeed, Snare argues that any discussion relating to industry and arts education must include 'the Earth' as a significant term in a three-way relationship. The various roles educators play that are constructed by various policy drives as well as their personal values are identified as a means of revealing tensions and contradictions. While arts education is operating within a paradigm that Snare refers to as the 'Industrial Growth Society' (Kvaløy, 1974), it will be unable to fully address the ecological crisis the planet is facing.

Huxtable in Chap. 7 employs a policy archaeology method (Scheurich, 1994), to analyse the UK's Teaching Excellence Framework (TEF) and its implications for music higher education. Huxtable identifies the TEF as an apparatus for industrialising higher education, including that concerning the arts. It is argued that the TEF embeds a neoliberal governmentality, aimed at entrenching marketisation and industrialisation at the expense of teaching excellence. The TEF represents one instrument within a consort of educational policies that seeks to devalue arts education. Where subject hierarchies have been drawn, through this 'objective' lens of graduate outcomes, music education has been negatively impacted with catastrophic effect. Neoliberal policy making has resulted in reaching a critical point of crisis for music education. It is concluded that it is now imperative that new measures of 'excellence' that recognise the value of music education must be reformulated.

In the conclusion chapter (Chap. 8) Broadhead finally considers some of the themes and observations derived from the six chapters that address the complexity of the industrialisation of arts education.

REFERENCES

Adajian, T. (2018). The definition of art. In E. N. Zalta (Ed.), *Stanford encyclopedia of philosophy*. Stanford University. https://plato.stanford.edu/entries/art-definition/. Accessed 18 Oct 2020

Alm, K., Melén, M., & Aggestam-Pontoppidan, C. (2021). Advancing SDG competencies in higher education: Exploring an interdisciplinary pedagogical approach. *International Journal of Sustainability in Higher Education, 22*(6), 1450–1466.

Atherton, G. (2018). Advocating for access: World access to higher education day and beyond. In S. Billingham (Ed.), *Access to success and social mobility through higher education: A curate's egg?* (pp. 225–236). Emerald Publishing Limited.

Baker, K. (2016). *The digital revolution: The impact of the fourth industrial revolution on employment and education*. Edge Foundation.

Bakhshi, H. (2020). *Digital culture: Consumer tracking study*. Wave 1 0f 6. Creative Industries Policy and Evidence Centre Led of Nesta. https://www.pec.ac.uk/assets/publications/Digital-culture-consumer-tracking-study-2020-Week-1.pdf. Accessed 08 Feb 2022

Banks, M. (2010). Craft labour and creative industries. *International Journal of Cultural Policy, 16*(3), 305–321.

Banks, M. (2017). *Creative justice: Cultural industries, work and inequality*. Rowman & Littlefield.

Bernstein, B. (1997). Class and pedagogies: Visible and invisible. In A. H. Halsey, H. Lauder, P. Brown, & A. S. Wells (Eds.), *Education: Culture, economy and society* (pp. 59–79). Oxford University Press.

Bernstein, B. (2003). *Class, codes and control: Theoretical studies towards a sociology of language*. Routledge.

Bhopal, K., & Shain, F. (Eds.). (2018). *Neoliberalism and education: Rearticulating social justice and inclusion*. Routledge.

Blackstone, K. L. (2019). *How do conservatoire graduates manage their transition into the music profession? Exploring the career-building process*. Doctoral dissertation, University of Leeds. https://etheses.whiterose.ac.uk/26037/1/BLACKSTONE_KL_MUSIC_PHD_2019.pdf. Accessed 15 Feb 2022

Broadhead, S. (2015). Inclusion in the art and design curriculum: Revisiting Bernstein and 'class' issues. https://lau.repository.guildhe.ac.uk/id/eprint/17356/. Accessed 03 Feb 2022.

Burger, C., & Easton, E. (2020). *The impact of COVID-19 on diversity in the creative industries*. Creative Industries Policy and Evidence Centre Led of Nesta. https://www.pec.ac.uk/policy-briefings/the-impact-of-covid-19-on-diversity-in-the-creative-industries. Accessed 02 Dec 2020

Burke, P. J. (2002). *Accessing education: Effectively widening participation*. Stoke-on-Trent: Trentham Books.

Cooksey, H. (2006). The impact of educational reform on the Wolverhampton School of Art. https://scholar.google.co.uk/scholar?hl=en&as_sdt=0%2C5&q=The+impact+of+educational+reform+on+the+Wolverhampton+School+of+Art&btnG. Accessed 04 Feb 2022.

Da Costa, L. (2022). The global context for widening participation in creative arts higher education. In S. Broadhead (Ed.), *Access and widening participation in arts higher education*. Palgrave Macmillan.

Denvir, B. (1983). *The eighteenth century: Art, design and society 1689–1789*. Longman Group Limited.

Department for Education (DfE). (2020). Review of post-16 qualifications at level 3 in England. https://assets.publishing.service.gov.uk/government/uploads/system/uploads/attachment_data/file/1002076/Impact_assessment.pdf Accessed 03 Feb 2022.

Duberley, J., Carrigan, M., Ferreira, J., & Bosangit, C. (2017). Diamonds are a girl's best friend…? Examining gender and careers in the jewellery industry. *Organization, 24*(3), 355–376.

Duffy, C. (2013). Negotiating with tradition: Curriculum reform and institutional transition in a conservatoire. *Arts and Humanities in Higher Education, 12*(2–3), 169–180. https://doi.org/10.1177/1474022212473527

Eatwell, A. (1989). Gordon Mitchell Forsyth (1879–1952)—Artist, designer and father of art education in the Potteries. *The Journal of the Decorative Arts Society 1850-the Present, 13*, 27–32.

Ferguson, T., & Roofe, C. G. (2020). SDG 4 in higher education: Challenges and opportunities. *International Journal of Sustainability in Higher Education, 21*(5), 959–975. https://doi.org/10.1108/IJSHE-12-2019-0353

Finn, S., & Fancourt, D. (2018). The biological impact of listening to music in clinical and nonclinical settings: A systematic review. *Progress in Brain Research, 237*, 173–200.

Forsyth, G. (1918, December 3). *Future of pottery industry. Mr Gordon Forsyth on the need for better design (to the editor of the 'Sentinel)* (p. 3). The Staffordshire Sentinel.

Gropius, W. (1965). *The new architecture and the Bauhaus*. Massachusetts Institute of Technology Press.

Heskett, J. (1984). *Industrial design*. Thames and Hudson.

Higher Education Funding Council for England (HEFCE) (2000) Foundation degree prospectus. https://dera.ioe.ac.uk/11531/1/00_27.pdf. Accessed 04 Feb 2022.

Hughes, C. (2012). Gender, craft labour and the creative sector. *International Journal of Cultural Policy, 18*(4), 439–454.

Jaffee, B. (2005). Before the new Bauhaus: From industrial drawing to art and design education in Chicago. *Design Issues, 21*(1), 41–62.

Jerath, K. S. (2021). The first and second industrial revolution. In K. S. Jerath (Ed.), *Science, technology and modernity* (pp. 103–118). Springer.

Kvaløy, S. (1974). Ecophilosophy and ecopolitics: Thinking and acting in response to the threats of ecocatastrophe. *The North American Review, 259*(2), 16–28.

Makridakis, S. (2017). The forthcoming Artificial Intelligence (AI) revolution: Its impact on society and firms. *Futures, 90*, 46–60.

Marglin, S., & Schor, J. (Eds.). (1990). *The golden age of capitalism: Reinterpreting the post-war experience.* Clarendon Press.

Miller, C. (2003). *Behind the mosaic: One hundred years of art education.* Leeds Museums and Galleries.

Nochlin, L. (1989). *Women, art and power and other essays.* Harper & Row publishers inc..

Office for Students (OfS) (2021). Official statistic: Key performance measure 4: Gap in degree outcomes (1sts or 2:1s) between white students and black students. https://www.officeforstudents.org.uk/about/measures-of-our-success/participation-performance-measures/gap-in-degree-outcomes-1sts-or-21s-between-white-students-and-black-students/. Accessed 28 Oct 2021.

Orr, S., & Shreeve, A. (2017). *Art and design pedagogy in higher education: Knowledge, values and ambiguity in the creative curriculum.* Routledge.

Palmer, J., & Dodson, M. (1995). *Design and aesthetics: A reader.* Routledge.

Papanek, V. (1974). *Design for the real world: Human ecology and social change.* Paladin.

Parker, R. (1984). *The subversive stitch: Embroidery and the making of the feminine.* The Women's Press Ltd.

Parker, R., & Pollock, G. (1981). *Old mistresses: Women, art and ideology.* Pandora Press.

Pevsner, N. (1937). *An enquiry into industrial art in England.* Cambridge University Press.

Pevsner, N. (1940). *Academies of art, past and present.* Cambridge University Press.

Pevsner, N. (1964). *Pioneers of modern design: From William Morris to Walter Gropius.* Pelican.

Quality Assurance Agency for UK Higher Education (QAA) (2019). Subject benchmark statements. https://www.qaa.ac.uk/docs/qaa/subject-benchmark-statements/sbs-art-and-design-17.pdf?sfvrsn=71eef781_16. Accessed 04 Feb 2022.

Read, H. (1961). *Art and industry: The principles of industrial design*. Indiana University Press.

Rogoff, I. (2006). Art schools then and now. *Frieze, Contemporary Art and Culture, 101*, 142–147.

Romans, M. (2005). *Histories of art and design education: Collected essays*. Intellect Books.

Scheurich, J. J. (1994). Policy archaeology: A new policy studies methodology. *Journal of Education Policy, 9*(4), 297–316.

Shreeve, A. (2011, May 18). The way we were? Signature pedagogies under threat. In *Researching design education, 1st international symposium, Cumulus // DRS for Design Education Researchers* (pp. 112–125). Cumulus Association and DRS.

Skilton, M., & Hovsepian, F. (2018). *The 4th industrial revolution*. Springer Nature.

Spours, J. (1988). *Art deco tableware*. Wardlock limited.

Sykes, J. (2008). A history of design and pedagogy at Burslem School of Art. In C. Hatton (Ed.), *Design, pedagogy, research*. Jeremy Mills Publishing.

Tett, L., & Hamilton, M. (Eds.). (2021). *Resisting neoliberalism in education: Local, national and transnational perspectives*. Policy Press.

Vasari, G. (1998). *The lives of the artists* (Reissue ed.). Oxford University Press.

Warren, L. (1916). The atelier system. *The American Magazine of Art, 7*(3), 112–114.

Watson, D. (2019). Fordism: A review essay. *Labor History, 60*(2), 144–159.

Whiteley, N. (1993). *Design for society*. Reaktion Books.

Williams, J. (2013). *Consuming higher education: Why learning can't be bought*. Bloomsbury Academic, an imprint of Bloomsbury Publishing Plc.

Wood, J. (1990). The socially responsible designer. *Design, 499*, 9.

'The industrious muse?' Commodification and Craft in Further and Higher Education

Bill Esmond

Abstract The place of subjects in curriculum is increasingly defined by their perceived contribution to student employability and economic competitiveness, with arts education repositioned as subordinate to creative industries. These issues are raised especially sharply in post-16 education, where discourses of practical activity and 'craft' appear favourable to creative subjects, yet these conform uneasily to norms of 'industry placement' in recent technical education reforms. On the basis of a series of research projects in post-16 education, it is argued that these developments reflect not outright hostility to the arts but their (the arts') complex relationship to the commodification of education and to greater inequality within this sector, across educational phases and in society. The arts, which provide insights and promote values that are a poor fit with much of the contemporary UK government agenda, have their own inequalities and relationship with social inequality. However, at a time of health, economic and climate emergencies, they also offer possibilities to rethink how the whole project of learning about work can contribute to a sustainable and socially just world.

B. Esmond (✉)
University of Derby, Derby, UK
e-mail: W.Esmond@derby.ac.uk

23

S. Broadhead (ed.), *The Industrialisation of Arts Education*,
https://doi.org/10.1007/978-3-031-05017-6_2

Keywords Education policy • Arts education • Commodification • Technical education • Work placements • Craft

Across a growing number of countries, the place of any subject in the curriculum of any educational phase or sector is increasingly defined by its perceived contribution to student employability, and to the economic growth and competitiveness of nations. England is among the countries where these tendencies have advanced furthest; one of its best-known expressions is a systematic if apparently irrational devaluation of arts-based courses in comparison to science, technology, engineering and maths (STEM) subjects in higher education (Marginson et al., 2013). Here, the Longitudinal Education Outcomes (LEO) graduate earnings data enables STEM subjects to be associated with student employability and economic competitiveness, whilst arts subjects figure prominently among those courses described as providing 'low returns', as in the recent Office for Students (OfS) consultation (preceding a 50% reduction in recurrent grant). This identified arts subjects as making a lower contribution to the government's 'national priorities' than STEM and healthcare subjects, which were designated as important 'for the delivery of vital public services, and maintaining the UK's position as a leader in science and innovation' (OfS, 2021, 19).

The developments are easily mistaken for the product of zeal for the scientific and technical, at a moment of crisis beset with phantasms of technological transformation, where artificial intelligence and an assortment of new technologies are presented as a fourth industrial revolution (Schwab, 2017; Avis, 2018). Such perceptions lie behind public defences of arts education that reference the creative industries' value to economic growth, employment and public finances or the citation of creativity as an essential prerequisite of innovation. Protagonists of the arts may feel a need to justify themselves in terms of their contribution to the national economy rather than their role in human flourishing (see e.g. Nussbaum, 2010). However, to see such attacks on arts, humanities and social sciences as responses to the needs of industry is to oversimplify the relationship between arts and the economic sphere. The positioning of the arts in contemporary policy as somehow counter to the needs of modern economy and society is a relatively recent phenomenon. For most of the period since the (first) industrial revolution, the arts have been regarded as intimately related to the development of productive technique, just as industrial work has provided subject matter for the arts. This instrumental focus on the need for education to serve the economy, depicting the arts as a luxury to be postponed until some future economic recovery, not only understates the contributions the arts make both to education and to work but misunderstands the direction of education policy in several English-speaking countries.

In this chapter, I argue that the apparent hostility of UK government policy to arts degrees and arts education more generally is not at all motivated by any ministerial preference for industry, technology and science over the arts, nor even by such broad considerations as promoting economic activity. However, it is the case that the arts fit uneasily into the elevation of market principles, demands for efficiency and the performance management of activities, certifications and teachers in recent years, which together have aimed comprehensively to reorganise education on business lines in several English-speaking countries (Apple, 2006). This shift towards more market-based systems and practices in education has a wider role in supporting the deepening of inequality in society that has affected all major countries over the last 40 years (Piketty, 2020). The arts in a general sense provide insights and promote values that in several ways seem a poor fit with much of the contemporary agenda of the UK government and its supporters. However, they have their own inequalities, and a relationship with social inequality that is reflected in recent educational developments.

The mutually reinforcing processes of reorganising educational systems and practices on purely business principles, along with the broader promotion of cultural and economic inequalities, are felt everywhere. In many ways they find their strongest expression not in higher education nor in schooling but in the further education sector to which, especially in relation to England, the UK government argues for a transfer of resources. Further education in England has been at the heart of public sector reform for some 30 years and is currently being reframed by 'technical education' policies associated with the recent Sainsbury Review (Independent Panel on Technical Education, 2016). These are notable for the requirement that young people undertake extended 'industry placements' to prepare them for the rigours of working life. Whilst the practical difficulties this raises for arts-related subjects will be self-evident to many readers, these tensions also reflect deeper ways in which the arts may come into conflict with contemporary educational and societal changes. They are part of a broader reframing of post-school education in ways that purport to favour those young people more likely to enter a further education college to pursue a hairdressing or engineering course than to enter a university; but which, as Liz Atkins and I have argued recently (Esmond & Atkins, 2022), is more likely to perpetuate society's inequalities than to heal them.

This chapter therefore examines the way the tensions between the arts and UK government agendas are playing out in this sector where the arts have traditionally been strongly represented and which now lies at the heart of education policy in England. The approach can be described as a genealogy (e.g. Foucault, 1997) through which terminologies and practices related to the arts and technical education have come together in recent years, ending with something of a mutual rejection. I begin with a discussion of the emergence of 'technical education' policies in further education, and their implications for the arts, examining contemporary policy claims to promote educational opportunity by way of routes that are supposedly more responsive to industry. I then report on how this difficult relationship between the arts and these reforms has occurred in practice, drawing on a series of earlier studies that include empirical data from arts-based provision. I then situate these policy developments within the tensions between the arts and a broad range of contemporary social, economic and education policies in several English-speaking countries, which are both driven and reinforced by the purposeful advance of societal inequality. From here I conclude that the main challenge that the arts present to such policies is not simply the practical disconnect between most arts-based employment and the somewhat 'Fordist' conceptualisation of 'industry placements' but the antithesis between the direction of contemporary economies and employment practices and the possibilities that arts education offers for a deeper understanding of the human condition.

Arts and 'Technical Education': A Brief Genealogy

The immediate challenge to post-16 arts provision lies in the curriculum and qualifications reforms described as 'technical education' and the 'T-Level' qualifications. This terminology may sound ill-suited to arts provision, recalling a distant past when technical colleges and art colleges were more often than not separate institutions (Venables, 1955, table 3). But post-16 education (once but no longer described as 'post-compulsory') has multiple terminological difficulties owing to its breadth. Tracing the pre-history of these reforms, Fuller and Unwin (2011) argue that:

the reappearance of the term 'technical education' and its juxtaposition with the terms 'practical learning' and 'craft skills' provide the leitmotifs for the way in which the Coalition Government is seeking to refashion the image and purpose of VET [vocational education and training]. (2011, p. 192)

The terminology of craft and the practical may seem less of a direct challenge to arts education, although as we shall see its eventual applications to the curriculum have been relatively narrow. These authors note speeches by Michael Gove and John Hayes extolling the virtues of skilled work and 'craftsmanship' with reference to recent American texts (Sennett, 2009; Crawford, 2009), Hayes going so far as to call for 'a new aesthetics of craft, indeed, a new Arts and Crafts movement' (Hayes, 2010), However, such concepts are not accidental; they play a role in the development and implementation of policy over time. The role of arts education in these changes has been little noted but is emblematic of the way these reforms have become increasingly focused on a minority of students.

The relationship of the arts to technical education may be summarised briefly. In the Sainsbury Review (Independent Panel on Technical Education, 2016), whilst there is no specific mention of arts education or institutions (except in a comparative discussion of Singapore), its proposed technical education routes include 'Creative and Design', ostensibly preparing young people for a field said to number 529,573 jobs. Typical job roles are listed as 'arts producer, graphic designer, audio-visual technician, journalist, product/clothing designer, upholsterer, tailor, furniture maker' (Independent Panel on Technical Education, 2016, p. 34). Since this review effectively proposed to replace all existing vocational qualifications, a suggestion occasionally repeated since but yet to be implemented, this wide range of occupations represented a wholesale replacement of an array of provision in art and design subjects and beyond. By 2019, these proposals had been reduced to three T-Levels, to be implemented as part of the final phase in 2023 (DfE, 2019). With 'Cultural Heritage and Visitor Attractions' now withdrawn, only a T-Level for media occupations ('Media, Broadcast and Production') and one for a small number of specialist roles producing wood, metal, textiles and ceramics products ('Craft and Design') remain. This represents a relatively small proportion both of art and design education, and certainly aligns poorly to what is generally understood by 'creative industries'.

The reasons for this evisceration of much creative and design from the programme go far beyond the inconveniences of accommodating the arts in the technical education model, although these are not unimportant as discussed below. The narrowing also signifies the mutual differences of contemporary education policy and the arts, which have both practical and moral dimensions. This suggests the examination of these developments through an approach that draws on Foucault's (e.g. 1997) concept of genealogy. According to the conception of several Foucault scholars, there is a turn from the notion that discourse operates largely autonomously of action (e.g. Foucault 1972) but that it draws also on changes to practice (see Olssen, 2014 for an extended discussion). In this case, practice is represented not only by normative practices in post-16 arts education and the industry placement model at the heart of the technical education reforms but also by the reframing of education on managerial and commercial lines discussed above. Additionally, a polarisation of society and its resources also finds an expression in technical education reform, with a separation of advantaged STEM-based routes from 'low-skilled' occupations, in which the arts and creative subjects are poorly accommodated (Esmond & Atkins, 2022).

In policy documents, the technical education proposals are represented as the product of brilliant innovation by Lord David Sainsbury and his team, including Alison Wolf who has authored a series of influential commentaries and reports in this area. In a preface to the government's *Post-16 Skills Plan* (BIS/DfE, 2016), Minister Nick Boles lauded their work and the report's non-political, pragmatic conclusions, as well as Lord Sainsbury's long-standing commitment to technical education. Whilst ministers praise the novelty of these ideas, they have not emerged fully formed from the heads of Lord Sainsbury and colleagues. Notions of strengthening educational practices both within the workplace and in preparation for work have been under discussion in policy circles even before the Coalition government came to power in 2010. Fuller and Unwin (2011) attribute much of this policy work to such Conservative opposition figures as David Willetts and John Hayes, derailed by Michael Gove and Alison Wolf's academic perspectives (resulting in compulsory maths and English General Certificate of Secondary Education (GCSE) retakes). Yet none of these innovations were created in a vacuum. Fuller and Unwin (2011) note the origins of policy discourses valorising the practical under New Labour:

> In the final year of the Labour government, the then Secretary of State for Business, Innovation and Skills (BIS), Peter Mandelson signalled to the

Labour Party's annual conference in September 2009 that he too was start-
ing to evoke the language of practical skills as part of a strategy to 'rebalance'
an economy that had become too dependent on financial services and had
neglected manufacturing. (2011, p. 192)

The notion of 'rebalancing' the economy achieved particular salience following the global financial crash in 2008. Hitherto, the policies of successive Conservative and New Labour governments had seen the growth of
services, and especially financial services, as more than adequate compen-
sation for the contraction of manufacturing industry. During the austerity
years that followed, such ideas attracted further interest, for example during Chancellor George Osborne's promotion of manufacturing. Notions
of 'reshoring' manufacturing became a key theme for the Trump candi-
dacy and presidency in the United States, although these were to some
extent outliers. The dominant ideas of international policy emerging from
the Organisation for Economic Co-operation and Development (OECD),
World Bank and others were more focused on the achievement of international competitiveness through work-based qualifications: and these ideas
have been further reinforced in the search for post-COVID recovery
(OECD 2020; Osnabruck Declaration, 2020; Avis et al. 2021).

The Sainsbury Review and Skills Plan expressed these notions in terms
of the need to imitate countries with stronger technical and vocational
systems, where apprenticeships involve a substantial period of learning in
school. The Review noted that:

in many countries with high-performing technical education systems—
including Norway, the Netherlands and Switzerland—there is widespread
integration across the two modes of technical education learning:
employment-based, such as an apprenticeship; and college-based, such as a
full-time study programme at a college. In England these two modes of
learning already overlap to a significant degree: all apprenticeships, for
example, are required to include at least 20% 'off-the-job' (college-based)
training. However the two systems have largely been designed to operate
separately. (Independent Panel on Technical Education, 2016, p. 24)

This international comparison captures an element of truth but nothing of
its complexities, and contains a degree of wishful thinking. In England, as
elsewhere, vocational routes are the option by which low-attaining young
people excluded from general education routes progress to upper-
secondary level; and here classroom-based curricula have become

especially diluted and generic. Moreover, apprenticeships and other forms of work-based learning, which elsewhere are seen as desirable routes, have become a relatively low-status route to which low-attaining groups of young people are directed, such as young women on care and early years courses (Young 2006; Atkins 2009). Compared to the 'churn' which young people on vocational education and training (VET) routes in the UK often experience, holding a succession of low-paid, low-skilled jobs before finding more stable employment at a later stage, several north European countries have more straightforward transitions and lower youth employment. These countries' school-based education tends to place greater emphasis on the type of subject knowledge associated with general education; learning at work builds on learning at school and provides more secure transitions to employment and adulthood (Pohl & Walther, 2007; Raffe, 2014; Emmenegger & Seitzl, 2020). However, the Review did not begin to propose any genuine policy learning from these systems, which would have required a substantial rebuilding of the architecture of education, labour markets and employment. The difficulties of constructing pathways, curricula, skills ecologies and learning networks that this might entail would be hugely complex and challenging (Keep, 2005; Esmond, 2019). Instead, classroom-based curricula were to be adapted to the especially weak model of apprenticeships in England.

Thus, although the Sainsbury Review argued that 'Technical education is not, and must not be allowed to become simply "vocational education rebadged"' (Independent Review, 2016, p. 23), the proposed changes centred on the addition of substantial work placements whilst college-based curricula would remain 'employer-responsive', now by making them subject to the approval of the employer-led Institute of Apprenticeships (and now also of Technical Education, IfATE). The essence of technical education effectively became the addition of placements to institution-based curricula and practices little different from those previously in existence. This is perhaps an inevitable consequence if the relationships between educational settings and employment are reduced to conceptualising the employer as the customer of educational institutions and custodian of learning at work. This partly reflected the desire of the UK government to assert further the dominance of employers over the education of young people in further education. This aim has been reasserted by the recent Skills White Paper, which sets out the priority:

that the substantial majority of post-16 technical and Higher Technical Education will be aligned to employer-led standards by the end of this decade. We will also give employers a central role in shaping the technical skills provision offered in local areas. (DfE, 2021a, §10)

The desire to assert employer prerogatives over education and training for this sector, like the blind faith that these are the stakeholders most likely to lead to beneficial change, is hardly new (see e.g. Unwin, 2004 for a reflective view). However, the centrality of learning at work to the design of technical education has raised particular problems for creative areas. The model of 'industry placements' itself reflected from the start notions of work that have more in common with the practices of mass production than those of contemporary creative industries. The features of the so-called Fordist production line, with a division of labour reducing occupational expertise to a series of atomised tasks and an emphasis on conformity to the process, survive into present-day manufacturing, as so many tightly prescribed 'production systems' and recipes for 'business process improvement' demonstrate. The same requirements predominate in contemporary mass services, leading to an emphasis on 'soft skills' that often amount to little more than compliance with team-based work processes.

These differences were already apparent to many in arts education by the time the Sainsbury Review was published and have since been amply demonstrated in practice. Empirical data from the period of their introduction illustrate these difficulties well.

THE CREATIVE INDUSTRY PLACEMENT?

Shortly after the publication of the Sainsbury Review and Skills Plan, a study of work-based learning in English further education (Esmond, 2018) reported the widespread use of employer projects as work-related learning opportunities on courses in areas destined for technical education's 'Creative and Design' route. At both further education colleges and successful private providers, problem-based briefs and practical projects provided by employers enabled students to work on real-life creative industry issues, often whilst learning additional technical skills to resolve them in college. These projects enabled an alignment between educational and work settings unparalleled by the design of 'placements' without definite educational purposes. One tutor compared his daughter's 'work experience' organised by a school to his own college's approach:

> She's got a week at Marks and Spencers: she's not interested in going to work in a shop but it's a placement and it gets her out of their hair for a week. [In his own team's placements] the ability to network gets people places, it gets people work ... where you're working with a client brief for maybe 12–14 weeks they get much more out of it. (Howard, course leader. Esmond, 2018, p. 205)

Ironically, the possibilities for exchange of ideas and experiences between college settings and the workplace outstripped the basic 'industry placement' design piloted for T-Levels but did not meet its requirements for an extended period in the workplace. Consequently, even though providers were wary of the demands that awarding bodies in general education made for evidence of academic achievement, both further education and private sector colleges were already talking of moving away from those awarding bodies whose qualifications would be part of the T-Level creative route.

These issues were further illustrated when the Department of Education organised their first pilots of industry placements in 2018. These were the first of three years of trials. Some adjustments have been made since then, to enable placements to meet organisational practicalities, but their lessons are salutary. Too many placements lacked clear purposes or opportunities to learn industry skills. A critical finding of the official evaluation of these pilots reported the way colleges prepared students for placements. This was overwhelmingly conceptualised as a process of teaching students to become 'work-ready': to learn how to work, rather than learn how to learn at work. Students were taught how to turn up on time, wearing appropriate clothing, take lunch, follow instructions and generally behave as required:

> Learner preparation activities focused on employability. The learner preparation that providers devised aimed to develop employability skills and attributes including soft skills, as well as to provide input on route or industry specific issues. ... The preparation programme offered by the national support organisation [the pilots had been designed by a well-known youth charity] was not intended to be route-specific and focused on employment preparation and employability skills and attributes. It also contained an option for a short spell of volunteering. At a broad level, preparation programmes covered similar themes—CV writing, interview preparation, generic employability skills. (Newton et al., 2018, p. 68)

The evaluation also included route reports that identified issues relating to the creative and design route, including the difficulty of 'micro employers' hosting placements, the concentration of opportunities to practice relevant skills in London and other major cities, and competition with undergraduates for the placement opportunities available. Whilst providers fell back on the strategy of employer projects (arguably crossing the boundaries of placement regulation) the difficulties of the labour market inevitably intruded:

> Learners were sometimes placed in the relevant industry but not in a placement where they could practice their specific creative skills. Potentially this could impact on their motivation and engagement with the placement. (IES/iCeGS, 2019)

Indeed, students in a wide range of creative fields have little to gain from the organisation of sustained placements even where this is possible. As teachers in a later study were anxious to point out, students in creative fields are more likely to need to negotiate a series of short-term commissions than to encounter the problems of integration into regular employment. Their experiences of employment are more likely to be characterised by short-term employment and insecurity than the discipline of taking part, for example, in the work of a regular team (Esmond & Atkins, 2020).

The expectations of such placements, underdeveloped at the time of the first pilots, are now summarised in work placement specifications for the remaining Creative and Design pathways, especially 'Craft and Design' (DfE, 2021b). These routes into what are often small-scale manufacturing operations with high levels of self-employment combine specialist administrative tasks, such as the specification and ordering of materials, with low-level, subordinate participation in production. This suggests a problematic articulation with the classroom-based curriculum. More importantly, it represents the limited range of transitions that will be on offer for students in creative fields. Whilst these qualifications may support entry to a small number of specialist practices, where providers feel able to offer them, these and the media pathway are likely to fall well short of the opportunities encompassed in the Sainsbury Review proposals.

Many of these issues are easily seen as practical difficulties, requiring teachers and colleges to find convenient solutions. In spite of the emphasis on employer-led curricula, the responsibility for solving such problems lies entirely with education providers. Yet the real difficulty is that such problems are generated by the requirements of a technical education that serves specific political and societal aims. In our recent work on the polarisation of further education (Esmond & Atkins, 2022), Liz Atkins and I explained the divisive nature of recent reforms, setting up new opportunities for progression for a minority of students on male-dominated STEM-based routes (the 'technical elites') whilst others continue to endure socialisation into the monotony of work routines ('welfare vocationalism'). Creative and arts routes lie to some extent outside this stratification, although the arts have their own inequalities. In part, they are accidental casualties in a realignment of technical and vocational education, fitting poorly into a realignment of post-school education that serves broader purposes. Yet the arts do not stand outside the unfolding of further educational inequalities.

Arts, Education, Industry and Inequality

The inequalities that exist in the arts, including those between possessors and producers, consumers and those who lack access to elite art and broader manifestations of culture are noted for the way that they are reproduced within educational settings. The opportunities that middle-class families have to build their children's 'cultural capital' (Bourdieu, 1984, 1986) provide important mechanisms to exclude working-class and other disadvantaged groups from more advantageous educational opportunities. This has been widely discussed in relation to unequal access to universities, especially elite institutions, and mediates not only choices and access opportunities but the way different social groups experience higher education (e.g. Bathmaker et al., 2013; Reay et al., 2010). The cultural advantages, including their exposure to the arts, which middle-class families are able to mobilise as a result of their familial and social experiences outside formal education, provide an important degree of protection against competition from students from working-class and minority groups. The latter are obliged to acquire the same forms of capital through study; and already perceive the most advantageous routes as places where students 'like us' are unlikely to flourish (Reay et al., 2003).

These rules, of course, operate rather differently *within* the arts and especially arts education, where society's hierarchies are accorded less deference. This has enabled a degree of access to higher levels of learning from disadvantaged groups that other fields have resisted. In the funding consultation on cuts in recurrent grant cited at the beginning of this chapter, the OfS explicitly pointed to the role of arts education in offering educational access to groups that are less likely to enter higher education:

> Students studying design, and creative and performing arts have the highest proportion of any broad subject group to have a reported disability, with particularly high proportions in relation to cognitive or learning difficulties and mental health conditions. They also have a higher than average proportion coming from POLAR quintiles 1 and 2. (OfS 2021, p. 18)

The participation of local areas (POLAR) quintiles are those areas with lowest participation in higher education and have for many years been targeted to promote 'widening participation' among young people less likely to attend university, usually those from poorer families.

Yet neither the educational opportunities for low-participation groups, nor the possibilities offered young people with disabilities, proved reason enough to maintain the funding of specialist courses. On the contrary, despite an unprecedented response to the consultation, arguing against cuts in arts provision, of all the subjects 'not among ... strategic priorities ... music, dance, drama and performing arts; art and design; media studies; and archaeology' (OfS, 2021, p. 17), only archaeology was reprieved (OfS, 2021). One interpretation of these cuts is that this is considered money ill spent on young people who, in addition to wasting money on unprofitable studies, are themselves undeserving, and failing to take the profitable routes out of disadvantage that policy prescribes.

This high-profile example suggests in turn that arts education fits badly, not only with the practical business of sending its students out to work but with the way education policies seek to address social inequalities. Just as in higher education, technical education policies offer to challenge exclusion by enabling young people to choose routes that ostensibly lead more directly to employment and meet industrial needs, rather than engaging in 'low-value' distractions on arts degree courses. These notions accord with broader conceptualisations of human capital and lifelong learning that urge young people to build their employability through the acquisition of marketable skills. In this sense, it is easy to see the technical education reforms as designed to provide low-cost, employment-oriented alternatives to university degrees, rather than to improve the prospects of those who do not attend. This deprecation of the subject choices of those deemed insufficiently economically productive prepares the way for a separation of arts provision, with the upper strata of higher education offering the arts to a privileged minority, whilst other routes are more concerned with mobilising creativity for the production of commodities.

Against this prospect, it is not difficult to see why the 'Creative and Design' route has ended up on the very periphery of these reforms. It seems likely that much arts provision will become separated from the technical education curriculum, unless funding levers are used as heavy clubs to drive it back. Yet this seems far from the possibilities that the arts have to offer to technical and vocational learning: the possibilities that critique and cultural breadth could offer not simply to reproduce our productive practices but to think the whole project of learning for work anew. At a time of health, economic and climate emergencies much more needs rethinking than the mechanisms by which young people learn about work. We need to rethink the whole purpose of working lives and work organisations, and how they can contribute to a sustainable and socially just world. It seems unthinkable that these purposes might be achieved without contributions from the sphere of arts and culture. Determining how such perspectives could be brought to bear on the future of education and work seems a more worthwhile project than either bending the arts to the purposes of commodification, or the separation of art and worthwhile human labours.

REFERENCES

Apple, M. W. (2006). *Educating the "right" way: Markets, standards, God, and inequality* (2nd ed.). Routledge.

Atkins, L. (2009). *Invisible students, impossible dreams: Experiencing vocational education* (pp. 14–19). Trentham.

Avis, J. (2018). Socio-technical imaginary of the fourth industrial revolution and its implications for vocational education and training. *Journal of Vocational Education & Training, 70*(3), 337–363. https://doi.org/10.1080/1363682 0.2018.1498907

Avis, J., Atkins, L., Esmond, B., & McGrath, S. (2021). Re-conceptualising VET: Responses to Covid-19. *Journal of Vocational Education & Training, 73*(1), 1–23. https://doi.org/10.1080/13636820.2020.1861068

Bathmaker, A., Ingram, N., & Waller, R. (2013). Higher education, social class and the mobilisation of capitals: Recognising and playing the game. *British Journal of Sociology of Education, 34*(5–6), 723–743. https://doi.org/10.108 0/01425692.2013.816041

BIS (Department for Business Innovation and Skills)/DfE (Department for Education). (2016). Post-16 skills plan. Cm 9280. Retrieved from https://assets.publishing.service.gov.uk/government/uploads/system/uploads/attachment_data/file/536068/56259_Cm_9280_print.pdf

Bourdieu, P. (1984). *Distinction: A social critique of the judgement of taste.* Routledge and Kegan Paul.

Bourdieu, P. (1986). The forms of capital. In J. Richardson (Ed.), *Handbook of theory and research in education* (pp. 241–258). Greenwood.

Crawford, M. B. (2009). *Shop class as soul craft: An inquiry into the value of work.* Thorndike Press.

DfE. (2021a). Skills for Jobs: Lifelong Learning for Opportunity and Growth, https://assets.publishing.service.gov.uk/government/uploads/system/uploads/attachment_data/file/957856/Skills_for_jobs_lifelong_learning_for_opportunity_and_growth__web_version_.pdf

DfE. (2021b). Creative and Design Route Example industry placement objective templates for T-Level in Craft and Design/ T-Level in Media, Broadcast and Production. Retrieved from https://assets.publishing.service.gov.uk/government/uploads/system/uploads/attachment_data/file/999028/Creative_and_Design_Route_final.pdf

DfE (Department for Education). (2019). T-Level action plan: 2019. Retrieved from https://www.gov.uk/government/publications/t-level-action-plan

Emmenegger, P., & Seitzl, L. (2020). Social partner involvement in collective skill formation governance. A comparison of Austria, Denmark, Germany, the Netherlands and Switzerland. *Transfer: European Review of Labour and Research, 26*(1), 27–42. https://doi.org/10.1177/1024258919896897

Esmond, B. (2018). 'They get a qualification at the end of it, I think': Incidental workplace learning and technical education in England. *Journal of Vocational Education & Training, 70*(2), 193–211. https://doi.org/10.1080/1363682 0.2017.1393000

Esmond, B. (2019). Continental selections? Institutional actors and market mechanisms in post-16 education in England. *Research in Post-Compulsory Education, 24*(2–3), 311–330. https://doi.org/10.1080/13596748.2019.1596434

Esmond, B., & Atkins, L. (2020). VET realignment and the development of technical elites: Learning at work in England. *International Journal for Research in Vocational Education and Training, 7*(2), 193–213. https://doi.org/10.13152/IJRVET.7.2.4

Esmond, B., & Atkins, L. (2022). *Education, skills and social justice in a polarising world: Between technical elites and welfare vocationalism.* Routledge.

Foucault, M. (1997). On the genealogy of ethics: An overview of work in progress. In P. Rabinow (Ed.), *Ethics, subjectivity and truth.* (R. Hurley et al., Trans.). Penguin

Fuller, A., & Unwin, L. (2011). Vocational education and training in the spotlight: Back to the future for the UK's coalition government? *London Review of Education, 9*(2), 191–204. https://doi.org/10.1080/14748460.2011.585879

Hayes, J. (2010). *The craft so long to lerne: Skills and their place in modern Britain.* Speech to the Royal Society of Arts, Manufacturers and Commerce. Retrieved from: http://www.bis.gov.uk/news/speeches/john-hayes-skills-and-their-place

IES (Institute of Employment Studies/iCeGS (International Centre for Guidance Studies). (2019). *Evaluation of T-level industry placements pilot.* Route reports. Department for Education. Retrieved from https://assets.publishing.service.gov.uk/government/uploads/system/uploads/attachment_data/file/916869/Industry_placements_pilot_route_reports.pdf

Independent Panel on Technical Education. (2016). *Report of the independent panel on technical education.* Department for Education.

Keep, E. (2005). Reflections on the curious absence of employers, labour market incentives and labour market regulation in English 14–19 policy: First signs of a change in direction? *Journal of Education Policy, 20*(5), 533–553. https://doi.org/10.1080/02680930500221685

Marginson, S., Tytler, R., Freeman, B., & Robert, K. (2013). *STEM country comparisons: International comparisons of science, technology, engineering and mathematics education. Final report.* Australian Council of Learned Academies.

Newton, B., Williams, J., Francis, R., Gloster, R., Buzzeo, J., Myford, M., Spiegelhalter, K. & Esmond, B. (2018). *Evaluation of the industry placements pilot.* Research report. Department for Education. Retrieved from https://assets.publishing.service.gov.uk/government/uploads/system/uploads/attachment_data/file/916870/Evaluation_of_the_Industry_Placements_Pilot_-_Research_report_Dec2018.pdf

Nussbaum, M. C. (2010). *Not for profit: Why democracy needs the humanities.* Princeton University Press.

OECD. (2020). *VET in a time of crisis: Building foundations for resilient vocational education and training systems.* Retrieved from https://www.oecd.org/coronavirus/en/policy-responses

OfS. (2021). *Recurrent funding for 2021–22: Outcomes of consultation.* Retrieved from https://www.officeforstudents.org.uk/publications/consultation-on-recurrent-funding-for-2021-22/

OfS (Office for Students). (2021). *Consultation on recurrent funding for 2021–22.* Retrieved from https://www.officeforstudents.org.uk/publications/consultation-on-recurrent-funding-for-2021-22/

Olssen, M. (2014). Discourse, complexity, normativity: Tracing the elaboration of Foucault's materialist concept of discourse. *Open Review of Educational Research, 1*(1), 28–55. https://doi.org/10.1080/23265507.2014.964296

Osnabruck Declaration. (2020). *Declaration on vocational education and training as an enabler of recovery and just transitions to digital and green economies.* 30th November. European Commission/BMBF (Federal Ministry of Education and Research). Retrieved from https://www.cedefop.europa.eu/files/osnabrueck_declaration_eu2020.pdf

Piketty, T. (2020). *Capital and ideology. Translated A. Goldhammer.* Belknap Press of Harvard University Press.

Pohl, A., & Walther, A. (2007). Activating the disadvantaged. Variations in addressing youth transitions across Europe. *International Journal of Lifelong Education, 26*(5), 533–553. https://doi.org/10.1080/02601370701559631

Raffe, D. (2014). Explaining national differences in education-work transitions. *European Societies, 16*(2), 175–193. https://doi.org/10.1080/1461669 6.2013.821619

Reay, D., David, M., & Ball, S. (2003). *Higher education and social class.* Routledge.

Reay, D., Crozier, G., & Clayton, J. (2010). 'Fitting in' or 'standing out': Working-class students in UK higher education. *British Educational Research Journal, 36*(1), 107–124. https://doi.org/10.1080/01411920902878925

Schwab, K. (2017). *The fourth industrial revolution.* Crown Business.

Sennett, R. (2009). *The craftsman.* Penguin.

Unwin, L. (2004). Growing beans with Thoreau: rescuing skills and vocational education from the UK's deficit approach. *Oxford Review of Education, 30*(1), 147–160. https://doi.org/10.1080/0305498042000190104

Venables, P. F. R. (1955). *Technical education.* Bell & Sons.

Young, M. F. D. (2006). Reforming the further education and training curriculum: An international perspective. In M. Young & J. Gamble (Eds.), *Knowledge, curriculum and qualifications for South African further education* (pp. 46–63). HSRC Press.

At the Centre of the Storm: Arts Writing and the Industrialised Curriculum

Karen Tobias-Green

Abstract This chapter explores some ideas about arts and industrialisation through the lens of creative writing and arts writing practice. When Tobias-Green was asked to contribute to the symposium *The Industrialisation of Arts Education* in March 2021 she began by imagining what the title of the contribution would look like visually—a dark, machinic entity, monolithic and yet clearly built by human hands. This image in her mind led her to consider representations of writing and art in general.

Keywords Arts • Writing • Industrial • Revolution • Education • Curriculum

K. Tobias-Green (✉)
Leeds Arts University, Leeds, UK
e-mail: karen.tobias-green@leeds-art.ac.uk

41

INTRODUCTION

Being a writer in an arts university I step into liminal spaces between text and image regularly. I have always been fascinated by the interplay of words and image and also the means of production of words and image—words in particular as a writer, but images too, as I work in a specialist arts university and am surrounded by visual and performative creatives. I began by exploring some of the ways in which writing and art have both bene-fited from, and resisted the pressures of, being mechanised and technolo-gised. I offer some thoughts and possible responses to the issues thrown up by these phenomena and I do this by positioning art writing at the centre of the storm.

The storm itself is the way I have chosen to conceptualise the industrial revolution/s (for there is more than one) for the purposes of this chapter. I am not a visual artist, although I do take photographs. I am a writer, but this place that I work in, Leeds Arts University, is my 'bread and butter' to use a colloquialism—in other words it is the place where, as an educator, I get paid, forge my career and find intellectual sustenance. It is the place where, amongst artists, I've honed my craft as a writer for the past 22 years. So, as I am a writer, I have taken some of the words that appear in my title and the title of this symposium, and they are 'arts', 'writing', 'industrial', 'revolution', 'education' and 'curriculum' and have begun to dig down into different definitions and ways of framing and understanding these terms.

This chapter is divided into four main strands. Section 'Introduction' explores the various ways in which language defines our world, how it shapes our perceptions of complex abstractions such as 'art' and how it has changed over time to incorporate socio- political, economic and cultural growth and change. It is by exploring the past history of language that we are most likely to arrive at a wider, more flexible and accommodating view of, understanding of and appreciation of our current ways of shaping meaning though words. Section 'Exploration of Words and Language' gives an overview of the industrial revolutions—so described as they are in fact a series of major technological, socio-cultural, geographical and eco-nomic events or happenings as much as they are a set, specific period of historical time. Given the totality of human existence, we move from pen and ink to printing press to typewriters to keyboards in a startlingly quick space of time, and our relationship to the words that shape our world is inevitably mediated by these enormous changes. Section 'Four Industrial

Revolutions in Relation to Art Education' looks at examples of art that speak to industrialisation, sometimes explicitly, sometimes interpretively. It is always helpful to visualise and realise the language we are using, to show images that reflect thought, speech and writing; and thought, speech and writing that reflect images. In Sect. 'Examples of Art Works that Embody Art and Industrialisation' I discuss and reflect upon the conceptualisation of writing at the centre of the storm of the technological and machine progress of often highly mechanised arts curricula, and conclude that the binary separations of physical and intellectual, digital and analogue, visual and textual are simply distractions from the real business of entangling ourselves with all the possibilities they can offer when we embrace them all.

EXPLORATION OF WORDS AND LANGUAGE

Opening up the vistas of that slippery thing called language, let us take a look at some definitions of art here. The *Oxford English Dictionary Second Edition* (OED, 1989) records that, as early as 1255, the description of art pertained to knowledge, skills and creative production as distinct from the organic and naturally occurring forms of nature. In 1558, in *Love's Labour's Lost*, Shakespeare—one of our most quoted and referenced wordsmiths—writes of the joys of art as both aesthetic experience and scholarship: "Where all those pleasures live, that Art would comprehend".

The OED continues the definition(s) of art as:

> The application of skill to the arts of imitation and design, painting, engraving, sculpture, architecture; the cultivation of these in its principles, practice and results; the skilful production of the beautiful in visible forms. (OED, 1989, n.p.)

This is the most usual conventional sense of art; art as a standalone definition. This definition does not occur in any English dictionary before 1880, around the time of what is called the second industrial revolution. I will explore the various proposed industrial revolutions further on in this chapter. This definition of art (above) was used chiefly by painters and writers on painting until the present century. And here is another one, also from the same source: "Anything wherein skill may be attained or displayed" (ibid.). Interestingly, the *Oxford English Dictionary* goes on to talk about art as something to be learned, acquired, studied and practised—a nod to the idea of curricula and to formalised arts education here perhaps—and also to the idea of art as artistry; the demonstration of skill, the mastery of technique, the clothing of one thing in another thing.

Then we have the free or liberal arts, as defined in the Middle Ages, and later the terms 'faculty of arts' and 'arts curriculum' appear (ibid.), ones we will be familiar with from formal education. Still studied at universities today and widely used are the degrees of 'Bachelor' and 'Master of Arts'. These are conferred upon students who attain to a prescribed standard of proficiency in these branches of knowledge, or, as these students are now called "graduates in arts" (ibid.).

Interestingly, both art and education conjoin here, and we have as an example the student body at Leeds Arts University. Here students study arts curricula; they graduate as bachelors and masters of their artistic and creative disciplines (most recently as graduates in creative writing and popular music performance). These definitions still pertain to the idea of the sensory nature and the corporeality of art practice, and to its aesthetic importance, whilst also referencing the formal curriculum-based nature of what we recognise now as our current education system, or educational machine perhaps. This foreshadows the idea of a fourth industrial revolution (IR4) which I see, overall, as a space where analogue and digital, text and image, body and machine, can exist and interact together.

Now let us take a whistle-stop tour of the terms 'industrial' and 'revolution'. I imagine these revolutions as a hurricane, a force of nature, a storm of nature and nurture, machinery and technology sweeping through the first, second, third and fourth iterations. The effect this has had on arts education and on writing is both tempestuous and profound. The delivery of arts education and the production of arts writing largely come through a formal delivery of an educational curriculum in which art is conceptualised as both a body of knowledge acquired while being educated, and as an enlightening experience. Revolution suggests to me not only the overthrow of one system for another but also the idea of revolving, turning, spinning, circling the eye of the storm.

Four Industrial Revolutions in Relation to Art Education

Research suggests there are arguably four industrial revolutions (Isa, 2020). The first began around 1760 and it can be signified by the process of change from a basic agrarian economy to an industrialised one, first experienced by Britain at much the same time as the USA, and soon after across the continent. The biggest changes during this period came about in the industries in the form of mechanisation. Mechanisation, whilst a boon to many areas of production, had notable downsides and massive impacts. Marx (1867) argued that it imposed control upon workers through the factory system, and that the speed of manufacture itself and the dissociation of the workers from the source and end result of their labour, resulted in oppressive practices and in the loss of individual skill sets. Alongside this, we need to consider the mechanisation of art and artisan work. Some rural artisan communities became quickly urbanised. Others, fearing the loss of their local knowledge, rejected the move to urban populations, for example The Cotswolds School of the mid 1800s, which gathered together artists who wanted to live a simpler life. They relocated to a rural location in the Cotswolds and used traditional furniture-making hand techniques in their workshops (Triggs, 2014).

Technological revolutions in design led to an increase in production in architectural materials such as steel and glass. The availability of these materials allowed for innovations in architecture- the building of bigger, more elaborate and arguably more aesthetically pleasing bridges, train stations and—ironically perhaps—factories. Mechanisation as art perhaps. The Crystal Palace, built in Hyde Park for the 1851 Great Exhibition in London, is probably one of the best-known examples of Industrial Revolution architecture. A largely symbolic edifice, built halfway through the century of the first Industrial Revolution, it housed the Great Exhibition and drew millions of visitors from all over the world who could admire not only the endless possibilities of glass and iron architecture but also the possibilities of—for some—a brave new world. The palace, designed by Joseph Paxton, displayed the finest inventions of the Industrial Revolution for several months (Johansen, 1996).

The second industrial revolution (1890s to 1940s) started at the end of the nineteenth century with advancements resulting in electricity, gas and oil, automobiles and the start of plane travel. (Coinciding with this, my own institution, Leeds Arts University, itself can trace its roots back to

1846, and the original Leeds School of Art.) The second industrial revolution, whether we see it as a part of a continuum or a related but very different phenomenon, involved the development of new methods of communication such as the telegraph and the telephone, and in the second half of the twentieth century we see perhaps industrial revolution three: the emergence of nuclear energy, the rise of electronics and telecoms and of course computers and biotech (Isa, 2020). The industrial revolution as a single concept located in the western world became over a relatively short timescale a global phenomenon affecting all areas of human life.

The magnitude of the fourth industrial revolution (IR4), which arguably we are still in now with the continued development of technology and communications, is yet unknown but it is exemplified by the internet, which has allowed mass simultaneous communication on a global scale never previously imagined (Philbeck & Davis, 2018). This continues to have a significant influence on every facet of life, going beyond industrial sectors to all other industries and agencies, as well as defining the way people go about their everyday lives. IR4 has of course had a huge effect on all forms of education, and my own university, a specialist arts institution, mirrors in many ways those changes.

The field of visual arts education and creative writing is directly and indirectly continuously shaped by technological advancements. On the creative writing degree, my students submit their work electronically, allowing enormous file sizes that contain images, sound and video clips. On fashion design courses students can create and realise 3D images and pattern cutting in a way unthought of less than 50 years ago. This reimagining of the human body in cyberspace not only encourages new ways of thinking about design, it allows new ways of reimagining the notion of human and body (Haraway, 2006). Critical disability studies and design have the opportunity to intersect in daring non-normative approaches to the 'normal', 'regular' human body. In fine art, the convergence of analogue and digital has led to a reconsideration of both (McRuer, 2004).

Now let us turn our attention more specifically to the definition and scope of the term art writing. In the creative discipline of art and design, students need to develop the ability to critically assess and put into words what they feel, think and know about their working practices and, by extension, their work. The careful development of the transition between knowing instinctively, thinking and writing is well established in literature (e.g. Biggs, 2004; Groppel-Wegener, 2012; Schön, 1983, 1987). Orr and

Blythman (2005) liken the process of design to that of writing an essay while George talks about a "tug of war between words and images" that can be "productive as it brings into relief the multiple dimensions of all forms of communication" (George, 2002, p. 14). Addressing notions of writing about/for art in the process of art education, I see writing as a tool with which educators can arm students as a way of making reflection explicit. It is like the mechanised production line, the ink pot and quill, the scalpel and the easel—both a means of production and an enmeshed element of creativity.

The writing process itself is for many of us both analogue and digital. It's a mixture of the free-form scrawl and the digitalised account. Technology has undoubtedly lightened the load of the art writer and allowed for a more economical use of time. Spellcheck, cut and paste, read aloud functions and synonym searches are a blessing and a boon. It is important that students of creative subjects see writing as a thinking process and developmental tool for their practical work, their art practice, their visual practice, their performative practice, their musical practice, their writing practice, rather than as an unrelated academic outcome (Groppel-Wegener, 2012).

The binaries associated with formal academic writing about art and the creative writing that comes from and is part of art are laboured over consistently in educational debate. My own practice and my doctoral thesis concentrate on the deterritorialisation of writing in academia and about art, and explore a radical pedagogy of transdisciplinary post-humanist approaches (Tobias-Green, 2014, 2020). Through my work with art students with dyslexia who write, I question the way in which knowledge is made—and by doing so cast a critical light on the notion that knowledge is in itself made, is a social construct, is the way in which power is wielded through who knows what and who is allowed to know what. I explore the manner in which knowledge relating to dyslexia is made and shaped; how knowledge around the primacy of orthography is made and shaped; how the educational institution is made and shaped; and how art writing might become a means of unsettling these notions.

Roland Barthes (1978) in *A Lover's Discourse* wrote:

> Language is a skin: I rub my language against the other. It is as if I had words instead of fingers, or finders at the tip of my words. My language trembles with desire. (Barthes, 1978, p. 73)

Barthes writes here with sensuality, with wonderment and with awe of the physicality of language—by which I mean thought, speech and the written word. He revels in the sensory nature of its effects. He uses desire in the way Deleuze and Guattari (1983) does, years later, as a positive manifestation of growth and change as opposed to a sterile and impotent yearning that is never achieved:

> In Anti-Oedipus: Capitalism and Schizophrenia we read Deleuze and Guattari's (1983) view of desire is not a psychic existence, not lack, but an active and positive reality, an affirmative, vital force. Desire has neither object nor fixed subject. It is like labour in essence, productive and actualisable only through practice. (Gao, 2013, p. 406)

Compare this with the description (below) of the process of drawing and feel the similarities.

> There's understanding that happens in your conscious mind which comes from taking in information. And then there's understanding that happens in your eye as you observe and in your arm as you draw, and that comes from the act of drawing. Feel, hear the creativity of the body and the physicality of mark making. Like writing, art and design have shape, texture, continuity, they have force, depth and structure. (Fry, 2017, n.p.)

So we see, looking at Barthes' exquisite, corporeal, desiring language around words of words and reading the above, that writing is both an art and a craft. The process of imagining, constructing and realising writing is very similar to that of the visual arts and involves both synthesis (the joining of materials and ideas) and praxis (knowing through doing). Technology may well enhance this capability, brought about by the industrial revolutions, giving student writers support, speed and the ability to save, share, revisit, correct and work into and out of text in a way that analogue processes sometimes can't.

One of the ways I work in my practice is to use tactile, sensory-based, word-generating workshops, building on the excellent work of Pat Francis (2009) to create cauldrons of thought, speech and text that interact with and play with images, materials and spaces. Because of this I am drawn to using examples of art work in my pedagogy, and this is no less relevant when discussing the industrialisation of art education than it is in any other aspect of pedagogical consideration.

Examples of Art Works That Embody Art and Industrialisation

Introducing art students to the pleasures and travails of writing about, with and for their art, I make use of visual images and artistic representations in all forms and media as much as possible. It is important that they see the language within the art, that they can think, speak about and write about their practice and the practice of others using words as part of the knowledge generating experience. It is in fact always helpful to visualise and realise the language we are using, to show images that reflect thought speech and writing, and thought, speech and writing that reflect images. I have chosen here an example that helps us do this, Elizabeth Price's *Felt Tip* (2018). Elizabeth Price is a 2012 Turner Prize winning artist. Her use of the digital technology associated with IR4 and her interrogation of the analogue, textual and mundane (ties being a near obsolete form of required work wear, a reference to a different way of working and being) allows us to explore the mechanical and the human. A former singer, she works in video and says of her work:

> I use digital video to try and explore the divergent forces that are at play when you bring so many different technological histories together. ... I'm interested in the medium of video as something you experience sensually as well as something you might recognise. (Price interviewed in Clark, 2012, n.p.)

Source 1 shows a still from Price's 2019 exhibition Felt Tip at the Nottingham Contemporary. This audio-visual piece—*Felt Tip* (2018) where shots of various business-orientated, corporate-looking industrialised environments are shown behind the moving around of yellow and green text references to a collection of her father's ties: he became, she says, quite obsessed with the collecting of ties (Clark, 2012). Here she curates her artistic interest in the simple yet poignant retrieved tie with the artistic obsession with ties, the stark industrialisation of the workplace and the office place, gender roles combining with a digital, almost 1980s type typeface into her 20-minute 2012 Turner Prize winning video installation.

The two-channel video projection, over six feet in height, a melding of pinhole photography, architectural interventions and an immersive video installation was described as:

> highly ambitious ... explor[ing] histories of work and technology by way of
> a ghost story and sci-fi in which a chorus of narrators from a shadowy near-
> future organisation narrate a story of memory and storage, by way of circuit-
> boards, DNA and woven neckties. (Nottingham Contemporary, 2019, n.p.)

In 2012 Price also became the first artist-in-residence at the Rutherford
Appleton Space Laboratory in Oxfordshire along with space scientist Dr
Hugh Mortimer, supported by the Leverhulme Trust. Price's residency at
the Rutherford (Invisible Dust, 2012) focused on solar imagery and an
archive of photographs scientists have taken of the sun since 1900. The
combination of artistic endeavour and technological intervention places
Price's work in that liminal space of mechanised art. Price's moving image
installation *Sunlight* (2012) rejects digital technology as a homogeneous
force. Instead she smashes technology and chronological timelines
together, using graphic design, montage, publishing, photography, sculpture, mashing up photographs of thirteenth- and fourteenth-century
sculptures, taken and archived in the nineteenth and twentieth centuries
and digitally captured and rendered in video in the twenty-first century.
This form of what she calls montage editing allows her to expand and collapse time and technology.

In the article, 'Industrial Revolution 4.0 and Its Influence on Visual
Arts Education', Badrul Isa (2020) writes:

> Historically Industrial Revolution is a process of changing the pace of pro-
> duction in the manufacturing industry. This change is due to the advance-
> ment of production technology which is from the usage of the old and
> traditional technologies to the use of the latest technologies. (Isa, 2020)

Artists like Price however refuse the chronological timeline of pre, post
and continuing industrial revolutions and instead provide opportunities
for a reconsideration of past present and future through this problematis-
ing of time and technology. Through the layering and compressing of
time, the presentation of time in parallel afforded to her by technology,
Price has a vantage point as an IR4 artist that gives her a unique opportunity to reconsider history. The internet and IR4 enable us to view history
and technology in different ways, ways that are associative rather than
chronological.

This next example is Carl Andre's *Equivalent VIII* (1966) (see Source
2), chosen because it represents the very building blocks of an industrial

revolution, yet in such a way as to be completely decontextualised. We walk around it, literally and metaphorically, and fill it with our own reflections upon digital and analogue, text and image.

It is 20 fire bricks, now part of Tate Modern's permanent collection, and what better example of the industrial revolution than the bricks that build cities. Bricks are building material, like text they are a functional material, not intended to be scrutinised individually perhaps, but appreciated as part of something larger, and so it goes for text. *Equivalent VIII* (1966) is equivalent to laying out individual words or letters on a blank page. Many pieces make the whole and many pieces can be haphazard or they can be intentional. From a distance it looks like one thing: everything is cohesive.

There are some comments from my level 5 (year 2 of an undergraduate degree) creative writing students who have been doing a lot of work around this kind of art writing visual symbiosis recently. I asked them "What is the work and what is Andre's intention?" "It has a practical intent". "It looks like one thing but it may be another because it uses the materials of labour" (which I thought was a wonderful comment). "Oh it's intended to be on this background It could be on a wall, or a podium, or a cabinet, but it isn't." "It's like Jenga blocks." "It makes external look uniform, the internal, that's different." "It's like writing something", said another one "all the little blocks are words that make a whole. But it you're putting the blocks together, it's hard to know when to stop. Like he could have made a square and then carried on to the rectangle, but who's to say that it's finished."

The creative writers I teach seem to understand what may be seen as a dichotomy—writing is indeed like the process of design; it is architectural; it is constructed. It can be what Fry (2017) said "Like writing, art and design have shape, texture, continuity, they have force, depth and structure". McRuer (2004, p. 50) describes the act of composition, of composing formal writing as a "performative act", the acting out of which we may feel alienated by. In formal writing, he says, formal language might not always come easily to us (McRuer, 2004).

The next example for discussion is Edwin Morgan's *Message Clear*, a concrete poem written about his dying father (1967) (see Source 3). Morgan's concrete poetry plays with the complexity of language and syntax alongside the human pull and push of emotion. This is an example of concrete poetry's relation to industrialisation and to technologies.

Interestingly, Morgan works with the typewriter and early computers—producing work via a human-machine interface.

> 'Message Clear' really forced itself on me as an experience. It was almost written involuntarily. That is most unlike the usual method of writing a concrete poem. It came to me in the old sense in which poems were said to be inspired. (Morgan, 1990, p. 59)

Commissioned artist, composer and producer Nick Murray (2021) went on to create new digital animations of Morgan's computer poems. Edwin Morgan's *Computer* is a series of game poems/poem games by Nick Murray and Antosh Wojcik on XMAS1. This project gives the poems a new life in the age of the internet, apps and social media. This is not a negation of the human heart, I propose, but simply a different way of expressing it.

The next example I would like to discuss is Max Porter's (2019) gorgeous novel *The Lanny* (see Source 4). Here Porter conceptualises sound, voice, performance, character and tone in a visual graphic representation of text. Interestingly, Porter talks lovingly of typesetting, of printing presses, of the overwhelming sensory experience of sitting in the London Centre for Book Arts in the East End, smelling ink and paint and metal and things being made.

> We are printing up sections of *Lanny* ... the sound of the print dances across the page. ... It's like concrete poetry, it's like a playscript, it's prose and poetry, it's letter pressing, it's a book about touch and encounter with physical objects. It's not a book that belongs to our time. ... It's not a book that belongs to the digital world. (Porter, interviewed in Harris, 2019)

"It is", he asserts "a book about people looking at books, and pebbles, and paper together and imprinting those experience onto them" (ibid.). Porter's fascination with the analogue and tactile reflects a preoccupation many artists and writers have—an exploration of the relationship of our technology-saturated lives to older, more obsolete technologies.

This evocation of print (a key facet of the industrial revolutions, making words available through mechanisation in ways never before imagined) dancing across a page, brings to mind again Barthes' trembling desire:

the formal inventiveness that will stay in the mind, the shapes and pairings, the sudden eruptions of imagery. It's the idea of Lanny's DNA as a magic trail shimmering through back gardens and playrooms. ... Porter's writing is poetically concentrated while also deploying a wonderfully common-or-garden kind of language, loved and used, rolling off the tongue. (Harris, 2019, n.p.)

The Lanny is a homage to the corporeal, tactile, noisy and richly scented world of the first printing processes and a surprisingly modern take on traditional themes of childhood, nature and loss.

This then brings us to writing about art as a tool for change. Being prepared to deal with controversial technologies being developed now is a future-facing challenge. Art and writing are necessary to build an emotional framework, to make sense of the dialogue at the core of this so called fourth industrial revolution. "Art triggers us to have ... 'calm, constructive and even uncomfortable conversations on the kind of future we want'" (Bandelli, 2018, n.p.). Conversations about these important future-facing matters often take place in a happy symbiosis of visual and textual.

The final example I am going to draw on for this chapter is Tim Etchells' G.O. (2015) (see Source 5). Etchells' practice is a hybrid of performance, visual art and fiction. Etchells says his work deals with:

questions of contemporary identity and urban experience, our relation to fiction and the media, as well as with the limits of representation, especially in respect of language. Working across different media and contexts opens up new possibilities and allows me to approach the ideas that interest me by different routes. (Etchells, 2021, n.p.)

Etchells highlights a key fascination of mine, the power and versatility of language. He says he is "drawn to the speed, clarity and vividness with which language communicates narrative, image and ideas, and at the same time to its amazing propensity to create a rich field of uncertainty and ambiguity" (ibid.).

DISCUSSION AND REFLECTIONS

This conceptualisation of writing is at the centre of the storm of the technological progress of often highly mechanised arts curricula. It's both a reflection of the advances of these revolutions and a call to remember the beauty and corporeality of the physical process of writing, as well as the emotional, intellectual, creative and psychological processes. There is not a binary between digital and analogue, between digital art writing and corporeal tactile pen-wielding, but rather an acknowledgement of the possibilities and symbiosis of both.

What came to me in researching and writing for this chapter, and as a result of the original symposium, is the idea of the sensuality of everyday life. So, we are talking about art and industry, but really this is a binary opposition in a way that is false. Can they both be understood through sensuality? If somebody is making concrete, if somebody is working in a factory, there is a sensuality to that. There's a corporeality, there is a tactility (Unwin, 2009). We cannot ever, ever leave our bodies behind, can we? Wherever we go, we take our bodies with us. Wherever we go, we take that, you know, that sweat that breaks out across your forehead when you suddenly feel nervous about something, that tickly cough at the back of your throat that interrupts the finest speech or whatever. We are our human selves wherever we go and I am real. I do not like binaries, I understand them and I explore them but I feel that we can, that it is a mistake to go down that path. And those young people going out into industrialised work placements are the same young people that will go to festivals and listen to music and be uplifted by it or watch a football match or read a book or go out with friends and feel something that lifts them above the every day. We are all of those things all of the time. Barthes (1978) and Deleuze and Guattari (1983) speak to this: even more so now in a mechanised and technological global culture: a coming back together of body/senses/mind that is so important to address.

As previously discussed, as an educator and writer in a University I am concerned with the question: 'Has technology democratised writing?' That's such a difficult question I think to answer. Technology can be used as a tool for democratising writing, yes. The pandemic and teaching online have helped many of us realise that there are ways of reaching students through technology that I had not realised were possible before and listening to the student body has been really interesting. This has not been a purely dreadful or purely wonderful experience, it's been an experience and it's an experience that we need to learn from, and take the best from, and I feel like that about technology too. For all its wonders, it also has difficulties and that is a human condition.

It is particularly important to remain ethical and student-centred when there are pressures to be more mechanised and technologised. Information can be so easily found, extracted and manipulated. Ownership, power and responsibility are often blurred lines. It is important to remember that wherever we put our thoughts, our ideas, our expressions and our opinions, whether that's in the personal physical domain or whether that's in a depersonalised, technological domain, that what we say and what we do has consequences, and it remains 'out there'.

Recognising the consequences of our technological actions may be harder than observing the consequences of our bridges, factories and railway lines but the remainders, the consequences of what we do, are always there, in the same way as carving into stone. Whether we do this in an analogue physical way or in a digital technological way (or most likely a combination of both), we need as creatives, educators, thinkers—as human—to be aware of our context, be aware of our surroundings, be aware of others. We keep our agency by making transdisciplinary the relationships between analogue and digital, art and text. The interface between text and image lets us collapse boundaries—writing and art become not interdisciplinary but transdisciplinary. Price, Andre, Morgan, Porter and Etchells use the power of image/text combinations to create a hybrid possibility that excites me as a writer and educator. The artworks explored here help us in some way to process all of the rapid changes we have experienced. In an age of storms, or revolutions, we need both images and text to help us make sense of things.

LIST OF ART SOURCES

Source 1: Price, E. (2012) *Felt Tip* (2 channel video projection) Nottingham Contemporary, 2012. https://www.fvu.co.uk/projects/felt-tip. 08 March 2022.

Source 2: Andre, C. (1966) *Equivalent VIII* (sculpture – firebricks). Tate Modern. Available at: https://www.tate.org.uk/art/artworks/andre-equivalent-viii-t01534. 08 March 2022.

Source 3: Morgan, E. (1967) *Message Clear* (concrete poem) Scottish Poetry Library. https://edwinmorgan.scottishpoetrylibrary.org.uk/1960s/south_african_outlook.html. 08 March 2022.

Source 4: Porter, M. (2019) *The Lanny* (printed book). https://www. frieze.com/article/max-porters-book-lanny-evades-easy-categorization. 08 March 2022.
Source 5: Etchells, T. (2010) *G.O.* (neon sign). https://timetchells.com/projects/g-o/. 08 March 2022.

REFERENCES

Bandelli. (2018). 4 ways art is sculpting the fourth industrial revolution. *World Economic Forum*, 14 March. https://www.weforum.org/agenda/2018/03/here-s-how-art-activates-the-fourth-industrial-revolution/.   Accessed 8 Mar 2022.

Barthes, R. (1978). *A lover's discourse: Fragments.* (R. Howard, Trans.). Hill & Wang.

Biggs, M. (2004). Learning from experience: Approaches to the experiential component of practice-based research. *Forskning-Reflektion-Utveckling. 6–21. Stockholm: Swedish Research Council, Vetenskapsr det.*

Clark, N. (2012) Elizabeth Price takes Turner Prize 2012 for 'seductive' video trilogy. The Independent, 3 December. https://www.independent.co.uk/arts-entertainment/art/news/elizabeth-price-takes-turner-prize-2012-for-seductive-video-trilogy-8376229.html. Accessed 8 Mar 2022.

Deleuze, G & Guattari, F (1983) *Anti-Oedipus: Capitalism and schizophrenia* (R. Hurley, M. Seem, H. Lane. Trans.). University of Minnesota Press.

Etchells, T. (2021) *About.* https://timetchells.com/about/. Accessed 8 Mar 2022.

Francis, P. (2009). *Inspiring writing in art and design: Taking a line for a write.* Intellect.

Fry, K. (2017). Learning from Lautrec: *The physicality of drawing.* https://www.lovelifedrawing.com/learning-from-lautrec-the-physicality-of-drawing/. Accessed 8 Mar 2022.

Gao, J. (2013). Deleuze's conception of desire. *Deleuze and Guattari Studies, 7*(3), 406–420. https://doi.org/10.3366/dls.2013.0120

George, D. (2002). From analysis to design: Visual communication in the teaching of writing. *CCC- National Council for Teachers of English, 54*(1), 11–39. https://www.jstor.org/stable/1512100

Groppel-Wegener, A. (2012). Developing academic writing skills in art and design through blogging. *Journal of Academic Writing, 2*(1), 85–94. https://doi.org/10.18552/joaw.v2i1.41

Haraway, D. (2006). A cyborg manifesto: Science, technology, and socialist-feminism in the late 20th century. In J. Weiss, J. Nolan, J. Hunsinger, & P. Trifonas (Eds.), *The international handbook of virtual learning environments* (pp. 117–158). Springer.

Harris, A. (2019) Lanny by Max Porter review – a joyously stirred cauldron of words. *The Guardian*, 8 March. https://www.theguardian.com/books/2019/mar/08/lanny-max-porter-review. Accessed 8 Mar 2022.

Invisible Dust. (2012). Elizabeth Price: Sunlight. https://invisibledust.com/collaborators/elizabeth-price. Accessed 8 Mar 2022.

Isa, B. (2020). Industrial Revolution 4.0 and its influence on visual arts education In: *Proceedings of the 3rd International Conference on Arts and Arts Education (ICAAE 2019)*. https://www.atlantis-press.com/proceedings/icaae-19/125941646. Accessed 8 Mar 2022.

Johansen, S. (1996). The great exhibition of 1851: A precipice in time? *Victorian Review, 22*(1), 59–64. https://www.jstor.org/stable/27794825. Accessed 8 Mar 2022

Marx, K. (1867). *Das Kapital: A critique of political economy* (S. Moore, Trans.). Scotts Valley, CA: Createspace (2011 edition).

McRuer, R. (2004). Composing bodies; or, de-composition: Queer theory, disability studies, and alternative corporealities. *JAC, 24*(1), 47–78. https://www.jstor.org/stable/20866612. Accessed 8 Mar 2022

Morgan, E. (1990). *Nothing not giving messages: Reflections on work and life*. Polygon.

Murray, N. (2021). Edward Morgan's computer. https://cassette-witch.itch.io/edwin-morgans-computer. Accessed 8 Mar 2022.

Nottingham Contemporary. (2019). Elizabeth Price: FELT TIP. https://www.nottinghamcontemporary.org/whats-on/elizabeth-price-felt-tip/. Accessed 8 Mar 2022.

Orr, S., Blythman, M., & Mullin, J. (2005). Designing your writing/writing your design: Art and design students talk about the process of writing and the process of design. *Across the Disciplines, 3*. https://wac.colostate.edu/atd/visual/orr_blythman_mullin.cfm. Accessed 8 Mar 2022

Oxford English Dictionary (OED). (1989). Definition – 'Art'. https://www.oed.com/oed2/00012468. Accessed 8 Mar 2022.

Philbeck, T., & Davis, N. (2018). The fourth industrial revolution. *Journal of International Affairs, 72*(1), 17–22. https://www.jstor.org/stable/26588339. Accessed 8 Mar 2022

Schön, D. (1983). *The reflective practitioner: How professionals think in action*. Basic Books.

Schön, D. (1987). *Educating the reflective practitioner*. Jossey-Bass.

Tobias-Green, K. (2014). The role of the agreement: Art students, dyslexia, reading and writing. *Journal of Art, Design and Communication in Higher Education, 13*(2), 189–199.

Tobias-Green, K. (2020). *Stories from an art institution: The writing lives of students with dyslexia* (PhD thesis) Sheffield Hallam University. http://shura.shu.ac.uk/27368/. Accessed 8 Mar 2022.

Triggs, O. (2014). *The arts & crafts movement*. Parkstone International.

Unwin, L. (2009). *Sensuality, sustainability and social justice: Vocational education in changing times*. Institute of Education, University of London.

Post-War Design Education and the Jewellery Industry in Yorkshire: Drawing on the Experience of Designer-Maker Ann O'Donnell

Samantha Broadhead

Abstract Ann O'Donnell, a designer-maker of jewellery, was educated at Leeds College of Art and the Royal College of Art during the 1950s. Her experiences of undertaking her work placement at Charles Horner Ltd are analysed to discover how successful 'educating designers for industry' was in practice. O'Donnell's story reveals a disconnect between her creative education and the conservative jewellery manufacturing context. In the 1970s O'Donnell started her own small jewellery making, retailing and exhibiting business. She also taught the jewellers in her locality of Leeds. It is argued she created curricula that were responsive to the needs of the local industries, whose workers needed training in skills. She also encouraged her students to be creative and imaginative, giving opportunities to those who could not access full-time education.

S. Broadhead (✉)
Leeds Arts University, Leeds, UK
e-mail: sam.broadhead@leeds-art.ac.uk

© The Author(s), under exclusive license to Springer Nature Switzerland AG 2022
S. Broadhead (ed.), *The Industrialisation of Arts Education*,
https://doi.org/10.1007/978-3-031-05017-6_4

59

Keywords Jewellery • Designer-maker • Design education • Education for industry • Post-war design • Charles Horner Ltd • Ann O'Donnell

INTRODUCTION

Briganti, C., & Mezei, K. (2011). Designs for living: Female designers, the designing female, this chapter presents a case study based on the education and career of post-war jewellery designer-maker, Ann O'Donnell (1933–2019), to understand the impact an art school education had on her subsequent experience working in the jewellery manufacturing industry. O'Donnell's experiences also illustrate some of the tensions between the curricula designed for teaching design innovation through making and the requirements of jewellery manufacturing firms.

Ann O'Donnell was a jewellery designer-maker from the North of England who was educated at Leeds College of Art between the years 1950 to 1954 where she studied textiles and jewellery as part of her National Diploma in Design (NDD). She successfully went onto higher study at the Royal College of Art between 1954 and 1957, specialising in goldsmithing, silversmithing, metalwork and jewellery. In order to graduate O'Donnell was required to work in industry for a year. So, between 1957 and 1958 she joined the prominent Charles Horner Ltd firm in Halifax where she remembers her contribution towards the factory production line. Ultimately, this experience did not fulfil O'Donnell's design aspirations so she continued her practice whilst teaching at Leeds College of Art from 1960 until 1986 (Broadhead, 2020). She was also an elected member of the Society of Designer-Craftsmen, previously known as the Arts and Crafts Exhibition Society, established in 1887 by members of the Art Workers Guild including Walter Crane and W.A.S. Benson. William Morris was its president in the years 1893 to 1896. The Society's certificate, beautifully written in a calligraphic style and embellished in gold, was proudly displayed in Anno Domini in Leeds which O'Donnell opened in 1970s with her business partner, Mae-Fun Chen. Anno Domini operated as a commercial gallery where exhibitions of international, contemporary jewellery were held (Norton & Broadhead, 2017).

During her teaching career O'Donnell taught jewellery design to local apprentices and also ran adult education classes in jewellery making. One of many significant moments in O'Donnell's career was in 1966 when her oriental style gold necklace with square-cut diamonds was chosen for the *De Beers Diamonds International Awards*. The judging panel included

Pierre Cardin (1922–2020) and Mary Kruming, fashion editor of American Vogue (Norton & Broadhead, 2017). One of the other winners was Andrew Grima (1921–2007), known for his innovative and modernist jewellery designs (Philips, 1996).

It can be seen from O'Donnell's history, education and design practices that she was working within a context steeped in the arts and crafts heritage where hand craft was valued and seen as integral to the design process.

While O'Donnell's story provides an insight into the tensions that arose between her 'art school' education and the expectations of manufacturers, it also illustrates how hand craft skills were assimilated into the manufacturing process. Later, O'Donnell constructed curricula for those working in industry. It is proposed that due to her gender and her association with teaching for industry she was marginalised within the art school during the 1960s and 1970s. This raises questions about the unequal treatment of teachers who taught part-time on day release and evening classes and the perceived value of that kind of educational provision.

The case study draws upon research that was collected from a curatorial project that comprised an exhibition, film and a contextual essay (Norton & Broadhead, 2017). It was shown as a retrospective of O'Donnell's work in 2017 where the exhibits were positioned as examples of post-war modernist design. Interviews between the researcher and O'Donnell were also recorded and transcribed along with informal conversations about jewellery making. Ann O'Donnell married Edward O'Donnell and had two daughters, Kate O'Donnell and Frances Norton. Frances was also interviewed by the researcher, and was able to give additional information about topics not previously covered in the aforementioned conversations, exhibition and film.

Context

Women designers in the 1950s had gained respect in the design and manufacturing industries. Forward thinking retailers such as Heals sold and promoted their designs in textiles, ceramics and furniture design (Briganti & Mezei, 2011). Examples include Ray Eames (1912–1988), Lucienne Day (1917–2010), Jacqueline Groag (1903–1986), Marian Mahler (1911–1983) and Brutalist architect Alison Smithson (1928–1993). Reinhold (2008) described a paradigm shift in post-war design against historicism, tradition and convention and pointed out that conservatism in jewellery manufacture continued to be more apparent than in other disciplines. Phillips (1996) noted that innovation in the jewellery field came from individual designer-craftspeople trained at art schools. After 1945 there was a turn away from austere industrial design and traditional crafts towards a more expressive experimental approach (Reinhold, 2008). Within the practice of jewellery making, goldsmith techniques were used but these were also experimental often being inspired by makers from other cultures like those working in Japan. Making techniques became more varied borrowing from other disciplines like textiles and sculpture.

Fine jewellery was traditionally purchased for sentimental reasons (e.g. to signify an engagement). Conventional materials such as gold and diamonds were chosen for their expense, rarity and preciousness. Dormer and Turner (1985) claimed that often the design of jewellery (as opposed to its symbolism and material value) was the last thing to be considered by manufacturers. As a result, much of the jewellery sold on the high street was conservative in nature.

During the twentieth century there was a growth in costume jewellery manufacture that was inspired by the fashion and film industry (Miller, 2010). Made with inexpensive materials such as base metals, plastics and paste, costume jewellery at its best was well-designed and playful. At its worst costume was a cheap and unimaginative copy of traditional fine jewellery; generally, it was mass-produced and sometimes poorly made.

O'Donnell's jewellery design did not fit into the tradition of formal jewellery made for women to celebrate key moments in their lives such as engagement or marriage. Nor could it be described as costume. It was design-led jewellery made with precious metals and stones but also incorporating other materials including pebbles, ancient glass or ceramic beads and even dinosaur bone (Norton & Broadhead, 2017). Dormer and Turner (1985) claimed that the consumers of this kind of work tended to be those working in creative fields who could appreciate not only the craft, but also the visual and conceptual aspects of the work. Jewellery was celebrated for its expressive and formal qualities rather than its intrinsic value and emotional significance. Consumers of this type of jewellery valued innovation, design concept, and the craft of making rather than the rarity or cost of the materials. Women often bought their own pieces seeing them as small works of art that could be exhibited on or as part of the body (Campbell in Oliver, 2015). People who wore the jewellery showed others how their taste was informed by discernment and knowledge of design.

The influence of the art schools in reinvigorating jewellery design innovation cannot be underestimated. A huge contribution was made by Gerda Flockinger an Austrian artist-maker, who established the first British course in experimental jewellery at Hornsey School of Art (Phillips, 1996). Ultimately, Flockinger along with others from Germany, the Netherlands, Scandinavia and the United States expanded the possibilities for jewellery design. The work produced by these people has come to be known as *The New Jewellery* (Dormer & Turner, 1985). *The New Jewellery* was a radical movement, greatly influenced by German designers with the opening of the Schmuck Museum (jewellery museum) in Pforzheim in 1961. Britain also saw in the same year the Goldsmith Hall exhibition which included 1000 objects from 28 countries, then described as new jewellery (Phillips, 1996).

O'DONNELL'S EDUCATION AND TRAINING AS A DESIGNER-MAKER OF JEWELLERY

O'Donnell was educated at Leeds College of Art in the early 1950s within the context of post-war British design. Modernist ideas originating from De Stijl in the Netherlands and the Bauhaus in Germany were beginning to permeate through the art school curriculum (Yeomans, 2005). This time period was pre-Coldstream, before art education became aligned with the qualifications of higher education. Much later the National Advisory Council on Art Education and the first Coldstream report (1960) considered that a two-year Intermediate Certificate followed by a two-year National Diploma in Design (NDD) was insufficient to educate professional artists and designers (Miller, 2003). It was at this time Coldstream created a new Pre-Diploma course (Foundation) and a three-year Diploma in Art and Design (DipAD) (Miller, 2003). During O'Donnell's time at Leeds as a student the NDD was a prerequisite to higher study at the prestigious Royal College of Art.

O'Donnell remembers that when she first started at Leeds she had anticipated learning fashion and textiles. However, when she realised that she could study jewellery making she decided to specialise in that. Her teacher at the time was a Miss Noble whose own style was reminiscent of the arts and crafts movement. After achieving her NDD O'Donnell tried, briefly, to gain employment and had moved to London, taking her portfolio around prominent jewellers to try and get a job. O'Donnell's future husband,

Edward, also moved to London; he was working as a musician in the 'Ken Colyer & his Jazzmen' band. It was during this time that she was invited to study at the Royal College of Art's School of Silversmithing and Jewellery due to a lecturer seeing her end of year show at Leeds. She decided to seize the opportunity to return to education (Norton & Broadhead, 2017).

The Royal College of Art was founded in 1837 as the Government School of Design. As has been discussed previously in the introduction of this book, the original aim of the Design School was to improve the quality of manufactured goods through the employment of trained designers and artisans. In 1853 the School moved to South Kensington where it evolved into the National Art Training School as part of the development of the area by the Royal Commission for the Exhibition of 1851. The title Royal College of Art was conferred in 1896, and the name suggested both the importance of art to design practice and the aspiration to harness art to industry serving the economy. In the mid-twentieth century the college began the teaching of product design and the provision of specialised professional instruction including graphic and industrial design (Frayling, 1987). Jewison (2015) noted that during the post-war period the Royal College aimed to train designers rather than craftspeople. Looking at Ann's sketchbooks (Fig. 4.1 and Fig. 4.2) it can be seen that she had skills in drawing and designing utilising a range of design inspirations. However, she was also a craftsperson and understood the value of experimenting with materials and techniques; this can be seen from her innovative use of gold and stone setting. O'Donnell explains her approach to design based on the materials themselves.

> The nature of gold itself is smooth and flowing when molten, or sharp and crystalline when cut or fractured, and this demands a certain sculptural, abstract form, and when it is combined with stones this is made all the more obvious.

Figures 4.1 and 4.2 are pages from O'Donnell's sketch book and show the ways in which she designed forms that were abstract and sculptural. This was design-led jewellery made in silver and gold and was in the spirit of the work produced by her contemporaries such as Andrew Grima (1921–2007).

Stylistically, the sketch book work is reminiscent of post-war sculpture, such as that of Barbara Hepworth (1903–1975), William Mitchell (1925–2020) and Eduardo Paolozzi (1924–2005). For O'Donnell the distinction between designer and craftsperson was not meaningful because

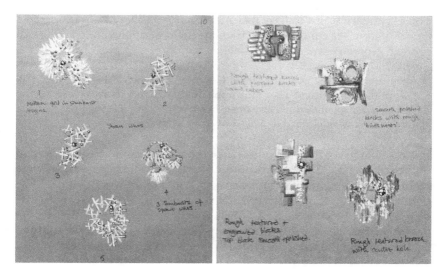

Figs. 4.1 and 4.2 Designs from Ann O'Donnell's sketch book from 1960s to 1970s. (Permission to reproduce given from the O'Donnell family)

the craft knowledge that she gleaned from making was central to her design process and informed her drawing.

O'DONNELL'S ARTS EDUCATION FOR INDUSTRY

During O'Donnell's time at the Royal College she was pro-active in seeking out opportunities for herself to study how the jewellery industry operated in practice. She did this through applying for awards, competitions and bursaries as noted on her curriculum vitae. Frances Norton, her daughter remembers that,

> Mum got a Royal Society of the Arts Travel Scholarship to visit jewellery manufacturers in Germany, France and Italy. It was a prize she had to apply for in order to win it. The Royal College wrote a letter of introduction, asking for her to have permission to look at all aspects of jewellery design in various factories abroad. She did this while she was a student between 1954–1958.

This experience seems to have had an impact on O'Donnell as it offered a model of how her education and training could be applied to an industrial context. Norton continued,

> She was inspired by what she saw in Germany. Designer-makers worked as part of the design team. They took inspirational designer jewellery and simplified it for manufacture. She came home with many German jewellery catalogues and subscribed to *Gold und Silber* magazine.

It is possible to see that, very much like the Bauhaus, under the leadership of Walter Gropius, 35 years previously, there was a clear vision of how the innovation coming from designer-makers could make work that could be transposed into an industrial context (Gropius, 1965). Avant-garde designs could be conceived of as being made in multiples rather than as one-off pieces. There was a role for someone with O'Donnell's design and craft training in the German approach to jewellery manufacture.

Industrial Placement—Charles Horner Ltd

O'Donnell, during her interview with the researcher, explained that a condition of graduating from the Royal College of Art was that she was required to work in an industrial context for a year. The certificate awarded to her in 1957, states,

> This is to certify that Ann Procter [her birth name] having successfully completed the prescribed course and passed the final examination in the school of silversmithing and jewellery to the satisfaction of the board of examiners, is eligible for the award of the DIPLOMA Des. R.A.C. on the completion of a further nine months in such employment as might be approved by the college authorities. This certificate, without the Diploma, does not entitle the holder to the title and style of Designer of the Royal College of Art.

The Royal College approved that between 1957 and 1958 O'Donnell would enter the employ of the firm Charles Horner Ltd, based in Halifax, Yorkshire. This enabled her to achieve the Des. R.A.C. awarded on 11 July 1958. It can be seen that O'Donnell's education was not recognised as complete until she had gained the industrial experience that the Royal College deemed was appropriate.

O'Donnell's daughter, Frances Norton, commented that:

The College decided on Charles Horner Ltd. not Mum, but they did look for a firm local to where her family lived. They considered industry experience as part of their students' education, even if their education had been more fine art focussed.

Charles Horner Ltd was an established firm begun in the 1860s as a manufacturer and wholesaler of jewellery, watches and silver goods, closing in the 1980s (Lawson, 2002). During 1895 the firm opened a showroom in Birmingham, the centre of jewellery manufacturing in England. Horner developed a line of good-quality jewellery aimed at the middle market that was manufactured not only with some handcrafting but also by mass-production techniques. Innovations such as plastic jewellery and giftware kept the firm going in the latter part of its history in the 1980s (Lawson, 2002). However, it was most successful during the art nouveau period (1905–1920). The firm was also known for producing thimbles and hatpins (Lawson, 2002). When O'Donnell worked there, Charles Horner Ltd was not as fashionable as it had once been during the early twentieth century, and was producing more conservative 'middle-of-the-road' jewellery pieces.

O'Donnell reflected on the decision to work with this particular firm. From her words it seems that she identified with the founder of the company to some extent:

> I was given a work placement at Charles Horner, Halifax ...it was very interesting how he got started because it was pretty much how I got started. Except when Charles Horner made his individual pieces he had one of those little suitcases like those people used to take their lunch in and he would go door to door. I never did do that but he probably did a lot better than I did because he did that.

O'Donnell was aware of the company's history and had an appreciation of the kind of skills necessary for producing the goods. She noted that,

> eventually his business grew and then his son took over. It was quite a good, big factory by then. During the war it was taken over for making instruments for the Royal Air Force (RAF) because there were fine workers there who could do that kind of hand-work.

However, although O'Donnell was interested in the history of the company and the enamelled pieces of art nouveau silver jewellery, she did not feel she belonged in that particular setting:

So, it was very interesting, there were one or two of the original enamelled pieces there. I worked there for … it had to be a year minimum, so it was a year—I left very quickly after that … [smiling as she said this].

It was apparent from the interview that O'Donnell did not enjoy working as a designer for this firm. And it can be inferred from her decision to leave after a year that she was doing this kind of work so she could achieve her Royal College of Art diploma. She explicitly remarked that,

My job was designing but I actually found it difficult for them to make those things [O'Donnell's designs for jewellery] as they had to be mass produced.

In a conversation with the researcher O'Donnell described how she was particularly critical of the silver hinged bangles, engraved with a traditional pattern that were being produced as being basic and unimaginative, requiring very little craftsmanship and creativity. This suggests that possibly O'Donnell's education had encouraged her to value creativity over financial concerns.

Norton remembered that,

There was a particular bangle—Mum designed part of it then had to make it, then do a time and motion study. Each of the jewellery makers was given the individual pieces necessary to make the bangle, they had to make something like 12 in a day—it was paid at piece-rate.

The company utilised O'Donnell's jewellery-making skills in a way she had not anticipated. The production process was timed to make it more efficient in the spirit of Taylorism and scientific management (Watson, 2019). O'Donnell's making of the bangle as well as other products was scrutinised and measured so they could be made efficiently on the production line. She remembered:

And another thing I was asked to do was to go to the shop floor and do timings—time checks for people to follow. So, the whole factory had to work to my time for doing a certain job. It was very tough because they would give me, say, a gross of medallions to enamel and it would take so many minutes and they would say "not fast enough—that would not pay—do it again!" And I would do it about six times before I could get the speed up that they would except. Then the poor work force had to do what I had timed it to which was. … I was not popular there [laughs].

For O'Donnell making was a crucial part of her design process. She was curious about the ways in which she could manipulate, construct and emboss metal. Figure 4.3 shows her in her workshop surrounded by her tools, some she has modified herself to meet her creative needs. Her method was intuitive and organically process-led and it did not translate well into an English industrial context. However, the making skills she did have were not used by Charles Horner Ltd to develop new products, but as a means of measuring the manual tasks in terms of time. This was a way of making the manufacturing process more efficient. This use of

Fig. 4.3 Ann O'Donnell at work in her studio; she is wearing one of her signature fibula brooches. (Permission to reproduce was gained from the O'Donnell family)

O'Donnell's expertise seems to have been dehumanising for her as a designer, and also for the workforce who would not have had her training or autonomy.

Testimonies from the workers were collected from Lawson's seminal study on the Charles Horner business and give an insight into the working conditions at the factory,

> Wages were low. Training was poor. Young girls did not stay long. The girls were on piece rate [i.e. Paid on their good output only]. (MS in Lawson, 2002, p. 19)

Another reminiscence from 'JT' confirms the lack of previous education and training in the workforce.

> I started in 1957 straight from school. I have both good and bad memories from my time at Charles Horner. The firm was run in a very austere, Victorian way. We were even timed going to the lavatory and they were mean with the lighting. (JT in Lawson, 2002, p. 19)

The accounts from the workers on the factory floor support O'Donnell's memories about working at the company. They give added insight into the way the company was managed with a tight rein on resources and time. The experiences of the workers also call into question how students from an art school background felt when faced with a way of life that was less privileged than their own, where the workers had less control over their working lives.

Charles Horner Ltd did not seem willing to embrace O'Donnell's creativity that could possibly have led to a more exciting jewellery line, which may or may not have been commercially viable. They were comfortable producing the more mundane pieces because they felt confident their target market would buy them.

The design team who were employed during O'Donnell's work placement had not gone to the Royal College of Art, but they did have some art school training. Mary Gregory was employed between 1953 and 1959 and had studied at Halifax School of Art. Lawson (2002) described some of her popular designs that were for 'staybrite' steel and comprised a swallow, dog's head and ballerina brooches. Margaret Eccles was there between 1958 and 1966 and trained by Gregory, but she had no formal training in jewellery design, although she did have a background of textile design.

Eccles' designs were based on photographs from magazines and had to stay within limits defined by production costs. The jewellery these designers originated was commercial and very pretty, but it was also conservative (see Fig. 4.4). The range of jewellery did not evoke the excitement and innovation that sprung from post-war design.

For Charles Horner Ltd jewellery needed to be made efficiently and economically. It is significant that many of the pieces were produced in the less expensive silver and set with paste stones. O'Donnell's approach of slow crafting was a complex and intuitive activity. Her artistic objectives were very different from the outcome of the timings which was to simplify the tasks so that those who did not have O'Donnell's education and training could reproduce them quickly. This means of production seems so at odds with O'Donnell's previous education as a designer-maker that it is not surprising that she only wanted to stay at the firm for a year.

Fig. 4.4 Examples of Charles Horner and Charles Horner-style silver and stay-brite steel jewellery. (Photograph taken by author)

O'Donnell's approach to design led to avant-garde jewellery pieces such as Fig. 4.5 and was dramatically different from the work conceived of by the Charles Horner Ltd in-house designers. Figure 4.5 is an example of O'Donnell's jewellery that led to her being selected as a prize winner at the *Diamonds International Awards 1966*, sponsored by De Beers Consolidated Mines Ltd. The Oriental style necklace was abstract, based on random forms that looked like they were derived from a mark-making exercise or experimental drawing. It was constructed from high carat gold and square-cut diamonds. The richness of the materials used and the complexity of the irregular forms would make it a challenging proposition to make in mass quantities. The piece was exhibited internationally, after which O'Donnell removed the diamonds and sold the piece to a private collector.

Norton explained that:

Fig. 4.5 Ann O'Donnell's oriental style necklace in gold and square-cut diamonds, *Diamonds International Awards 1966*, sponsored by De Beers Consolidated Mines Ltd (Permission to reproduce was gained from the O'Donnell family)

The job was not who she was as a creative maker. She had very little creative freedom. She did some design but it was with strict parameters. Mum was always commenting on the many Scottie dogs with jewel eyes that were made.

They were very tight with materials—at College there was lots of solder and students could use it willy-nilly [without direction or planning; haphazardly]. Charles Horner pre-cut the solder you had to use only was given for a particular job. Borax used as a flux for soldering was restricted to very small amounts.

In spite of all the challenges O'Donnell experienced at Charles Horner, Norton believed her mother had got a lot out of the experience Even though the business model was very different from the one she would pursue as a designer-maker undertaking commissions for bespoke pieces of jewellery.

She learned how to organise a work space, how to structure a working day, how to run a business. Security—how to keep everything secure when working with precious materials that are desirable. Craft jewellers used suede cloth to catch the gold filings from the making process so they could be re-melted, but Charles Horner Ltd needed something more efficient so nothing was wasted.

It is possible to surmise that O'Donnell's experience at Charles Horner Ltd was very different from what she observed during her visit to Germany. It could be argued that her educational experience had not prepared her for the need to think about the sustainability of materials and economic implications of not using resources carefully. Even a designer-maker, who does not work in an industrial context, needs to think about the practicalities, ethics and cost of their silver, gold and stones.

O'Donnell as an Educator for Industry

O'Donnell, being disillusioned with manufacturing jewellery on a large scale, returned to Leeds College of Art to teach in 1960, (she had previously, taught at Leeds with Harry Thurbon (1915–1985) in the late 1950s when she was also studying at the Royal College) (Broadhead, 2020). O'Donnell's employment was in teaching community courses, in outreach provision around the city and in part-time Business and Technology Education Council (BTEC) and City and Guilds vocational skills courses (Broadhead, 2020). In particular she taught apprentices from the local

Jewellery businesses. O'Donnell was able to teach with her husband Edward O'Donnell and they referred to their students as 'the trade boys'. Her daughter explained,

> Both Mum and Dad taught jewellers from local firms and chains such as 'Ratner's'. They taught a course called 'Day-Tec' which was a day release course teaching technical skills to those in the trade. Other courses included a Diploma in Jewellery and a BTEC. Dad let Mum design the curriculum and they shared the teaching between them.

Developed in the 1970s the Design and Art Technical Education Council (DATEC) created technical qualifications which later became BTEC courses. O'Donnell took responsibility for designing curricula suitable for the local jewellery industries. However, she also believed that her students should receive a well-rounded education and be encouraged to become expressive and experimental alongside learning the technical skills associated with jewellery making.

> Mum would create a curriculum where Dad would teach the technical skills like engraving and diamond setting. She would cover design history, design illustration, and design education. Mum would teach the more creative content although she did know how to do diamond setting.

O'Donnell was not only teaching them the craft of jewellery making but also the design process.

> Mum would teach them how to work with many variations of design. How to take a single idea then create 100s of variations—first through sketching, then paint up, then through making a mock-up out of cheaper material such as copper. She taught them that you never made just one of anything but made variations—a set.

When looking back to the images in O'Donnell's sketch books (Fig. 4.1 and Fig. 4.2) it can be seen that she was transmitting the approach to design she had developed through her own education and practice. Through the curriculum planning and teaching methods the students were being exposed to strategies that would enhance their creativity as well as their technical aptitude.

She would teach by trouble-shooting. If a student was stuck on a technical bit she would show them how to overcome it. She would show them how to create loops, fixings and pins, and how to add decoration without spoiling the whole piece. Sometimes they had to take the whole piece apart and start again. This was practice-based learning through pulling things apart to see what had gone wrong.

This explanation from O'Donnell's daughter reveals how craft teaching also develops approaches to problem-solving that would be beneficial for those working in small independent jewellery shops in the local area. Customers bringing in repairs could have them dealt with in their local shops, avoiding having to send them away to larger firms at greater cost and time. O'Donnell's courses appeared to promote a pragmatic practicality along with an aspirational creativity. The curricula were greatly inspired by the local area. Norton commented that,

They [Ann and Edward O'Donnell] also worked with the family-owned South Asian Jewellery Shops and became great friends with staff and owners. They had a great working relationship because families appreciated the skills and knowledge that Mum and Dad had. So, they could work in connection with family knowledge and cultural ways of making jewellery.

O'Donnell's curricula were flexible to meet the needs of different small-scale businesses and those working in larger jewellery shops or chains. However, to what extent her approach to training would suit those working in manufacturing firms such as Charles Horner Ltd is open to question.

O'Donnell's accomplishments in her jewellery design have been noted elsewhere (Norton & Broadhead, 2017). However, her teaching practice had a massive impact on local people who still remember her fondly (Leeds Arts University, 2019). Although her expertise was recognised through her work as an external moderator for Sir John Cass Technical Institute College and BTEC, teachers such as O'Donnell and Pam Rex (1929–2007) a potter and fine artist, were not always valued by their institution, spending their careers teaching part-time and in the evenings (Broadhead, 2020). Unfortunately, although cherished by their students these part-time teaching roles did not enable women art educators access to the networks, status and acknowledgement of their male colleagues (Kalleberg & Reskin, 1995; Kropf, 2001; Moen & Roehling, 2005; Webber & Williams, 2008). The perceived lower status of these kind of job roles also raises the question: to what extent did colleges value those courses designed for local industries?

DISCUSSION

In the 1950s there was encouragement for British art and design students to engage with industry. The Royal College of Art made industrial experience a requirement for attaining their design diplomas. The Royal Society of Arts (RSA) provided travel scholarships for talented designers to visit manufactures in America and in Europe. The RSA also managed Industrial Art Bursaries Competitions (IABCs) and related exhibitions that were open to all design students (IABC, 1958). O'Donnell clearly had a positive outlook on learning from jewellery manufacturers, especially from what was happening in Germany.

However, there seems to be a reticence from some industrial managers to fully embrace the innovative ideas coming out of design schools such as the Royal College. During O'Donnell's work placement it was as if her creative talent needed to be stymied by the economic rationalism and austerity of the workplace. Although she did learn many things from the experience, she did not feel as though she belonged there. Was Charles Horner Ltd simply a bad choice, made because it was geographically near where O'Donnell's family was based in Yorkshire and not because it suited her approach to design?

The Royal College and Leeds College of Art had educated O'Donnell to be an accomplished designer-maker who could innovate and push the boundaries of her discipline. It seems that someone with this expertise could be useful in a manufacturing context, elevating the quality and style of the product, but the mechanism for how this could work in practice seems to have eluded some British companies. O'Donnell's experiences confirm some of the criticisms Read (1961) and Pevsner (1964) aimed at British industrialists for not embracing innovative design as part of the manufacturing process.

The industrial context did contribute some valuable work-based knowledge that had not been addressed at the Royal College. The need to manage and be mindful of the work space, the equipment, time on task and the materials were all established in O'Donnell's time at Charles Horner.

It was of note that O'Donnell's contribution to Charles Horner was not her design ability but her skill. It was her technical proficiency and speed that was used to set a standard that other workers had to follow. The irony is that the Royal College aimed to produce designers rather than craftspeople, although O'Donnell herself saw the roles as integrated. Implicit within O'Donnell's interview was a discomfort with the time management part of her role. She empathised with the people who had to quickly make up items such as the bangle as they were only paid per piece.

Later on, in her career, after graduating, O'Donnell with her husband taught people who would be working in local small businesses as well as larger firms. They engaged with the local jewellery industry to develop pragmatic educational programmes that were fit for purpose, but also enabled people to develop their own design and creative lives if they wished.

Part-time, adult education as well as day release work-based programmes enabled O'Donnell's students to access jewellery-making materials, equipment and tuition. The importance of these modes of education for under-represented groups in the jewellery industry was illuminated by Duberley et al.'s (2017) research into the gendered and stratified employment patterns of Birmingham's Jewellery Quarter.

Duberley et al. (2017) also found the division of labour in the jewellery industry was based on a segregation between those considered as artists and those considered as skilled craftspeople (Banks, 2010; Hughes, 2012). This was echoed in the O'Donnells' own distribution of teaching where Edward undertook the training of students in the more technical, traditional, hands-on curriculum areas, perceived as 'male work' (Simpson et al., 2014). Ann's tutorage was in the area of creativity and imagination, assumed to be primarily the domain of women (Henry, 2009).

O'Donnell's career mirrored that of her of her students. She had, in effect, a portfolio career (Cawsey et al., 1995) where she balanced her own practice with running a jewellery retail and exhibition space, Anno Domini (1972–1978) and her teaching practice. Męczyński (2019) found that this mode of working was also common in the Birmingham Jewellery Quarter and in the jewellery centres in Leipzig and Poznań. Alongside this busy life O'Donnell also had the responsibilities of motherhood. Working long term in an industrial context such as Charles Horner Ltd would not have provided O'Donnell with the flexibility to undertake all these diverse roles. Buckley (1986) has explained that women's relationship to industrial design was seen as problematic as it contradicted dominant discourses about femininity. Also, on a practical level women, including O'Donnell have needed to juggle their many roles. Buckley (1998) has shown how women needed to manage their small businesses such as dress-making within their homes in order to manage their creativity as well as their domestic responsibilities. O'Donnell when she closed her shop in the late 1970s moved her workshop next to her kitchen so she could continue her practice.

CONCLUSION

O'Donnell's story reveals the complex relationship art education had with industry during the post-war era. The curricula in arts schools in the 1950s provided Britain with a range of exciting innovative designers, many of whom were women (Reinhold, 2008). Designer-makers of jewellery were well prepared to create their own stylish and desirable pieces, often based on bespoke commissions. Phillips (1996) noted that many opened up their own small businesses and commercial galleries such as Electron in London (Chadour-Sampson & Hosegood, 2016).

What can be inferred from O'Donnell's story was that in spite of public art schools intending to serve industry, there was not always full-consideration for the conditions and constraints of the manufacturing context. O'Donnell did not seem prepared for the need to manage time and resources nor did she design jewellery that could be easily mass-produced. It is also possible that she did not share the same values as the Charles Horner firm in relation to how the workers were treated.

Another aspect that underpins O'Donnell's experience is a hierarchy in the 1950s art school between artistic, experimental design and the technical, commercial, skills-based training. It can be seen that the art school valued the first activity, whereas the industrial employer valued the latter.

The ways in which designer-makers could contribute towards industry does not seem to have been fully resolved in the curriculum either. In O'Donnell's story the difference in cultures between the College and her work placement seems to have been very stark. This calls into question how students were assigned work placements; was it based on the location of the business or whether it could make use of the students' design aspirations? To what extent were firms open to taking a risk on making innovative new forms that potentially could revitalise the business or negatively impact on it? In spite of O'Donnell not feeling that she belonged on her work placement, she did learn a lot from Charles Horner Ltd about managing a work space and the need to be prudent in relation to times and materials.

O'Donnell was a successful and recognised jewellery-maker; however, her relationship to the design industry was mediated not only by her art school education but also by her gender. This can be seen in her subsequent part-time teaching roles that enabled her to continue with her creative work and fulfil the responsibilities of motherhood.

Although O'Donnell ran her own jewellery-making business and did not work with a large-scale manufacturer again after her work placement, she did go onto design curricula for training jewellers from local firms in the Leeds area. O'Donnell and her husband, Edward, did seem to have a close relationship with the local jewellery trade and were able to provide a pragmatic, purposeful and responsive learning experience for new jewellers from neighbouring and diverse communities.

REFERENCES

Banks, M. (2010). Craft labour and creative industries. *International Journal of Cultural Policy, 16*(3), 305–321.

Briganti, C., & Mezei, K. (2011). Designs for living: Female designers, the designing female, modernism and the middlebrow. *Modernist Cultures, 6*(1), 155–177.

Broadhead, S. (2020). Celebrating women arts educators on International Women's Day. https://www.leeds-art.ac.uk/news-events/blog/celebrating-women-arts-educators-on-international-womens-day/. Accessed 18 Feb 2022.

Buckley, C. (1986). Made in patriarchy: Toward a feminist analysis of women and design. *Design Issues, 3*(2), 3–14.

Buckley, C. (1998). On the margins: Theorizing the history and significance of making and designing clothes at home. *Journal of Design History, 11*(2), 157–171.

Cawsey, T., Deszca, G., & Mazerolle, M. (1995). The portfolio career as a response to a changing job market. *Journal of Career Planning and Employment, 56*(1), 41–46.

Chadour-Sampson, B., & Hosegood, J. (2016). *Barbara cartlidge and electrum gallery*. Arnoldsche Art Publishers.

Dormer, P., & Turner, R. (1985). *The new jewellery: Trends and traditions*. Thames and Hudson Ltd..

Duberley, J., Carrigan, M., Ferreira, J., & Bosangit, C. (2017). Diamonds are a girl's best friend...? Examining gender and careers in the jewellery industry. *Organization, 24*(3), 355–376.

Frayling, C. (1987). *The Royal College of Art: One hundred and fifty years of art and design*. Barrie and Jenkins.

Gropius, W. (1965). *The new architecture and the Bauhaus*. Massachusetts Institute of Technology Press.

Henry, C. (2009). Women and the creative industries: Exploring the popular appeal. *Creative Industries Journal, 2*(2), 143–160.

Hughes, C. (2012). Gender, craft labour and the creative sector. *International Journal of Cultural Policy, 18*(4), 439–454.

Industrial Art Bursaries Competitions (IABC). (1958). *Journal of the Royal Society of Arts, 106*(5020), 228–236. http://www.jstor.org/stable/41366234. Accessed 18 Feb 2022

Jewison, D. (2015). *Policy and practice: Design education in England from 1837–1992, with particular reference to furniture courses at Birmingham, Leicester and the Royal College of Art.* Doctoral dissertation, De Montfort University. https://core.ac.uk/download/pdf/228183592.pdf. Accessed 18 Feb 2022

Kalleberg, A. L., & Reskin, B. F. (1995). Gender differences in promotion in the United States and Norway. *Research in Social Stratification and Mobility, 14*, 237–264.

Kropf, M. B. (2001). Part-time work arrangements and the corporation: A dynamic interaction. In R. Hertz & N. L. Marshall (Eds.), *Working families: The transformation of the American Home* (pp. 152–167). University of California Press.

Lawson, T. (2002). *Charles Horner of Halifax: A celebration of his life and work.* GML Publishing.

Leeds Arts University. (2019). Remembering Ann O'Donnell. https://www.leeds-art.ac.uk/news-events/news/remembering-ann-odonnell/. Accessed 18 Feb 2022.

Męczyński, M. (2019). Work precarity of the creative class – The case studies of Birmingham, Leipzig and Poznań. *Acta Geographica Universitatis Comenianae, 63*(2), 137–156.

Miller, C. (2003). *Behind the mosaic: One hundred years of art education.* Leeds Museums and Galleries.

Miller, J. (2010). *Costume jewellery.* Mitchell Beazley.

Moen, P., & Roehling, P. (2005). *The career mystique.* Rowman & Littlefield.

Norton, F., & Broadhead, S. (2017). Ann O'Donnell modernist jeweller. https://lau.repository.guildhe.ac.uk/id/eprint/17303/. Accessed 18 Feb 2022.

Oliver, S. (Ed.). (2015). *I am here: Portable art, wearable objects, jewellery since the 1970s.* Crafts Council.

Pevsner, N. (1964). *Pioneers of modern design: From William. Morris to Walter Gropius.* Pelican.

Phillips, C. (1996). *Jewellery: From antiquity to present.* Thames and Hudson.

Read, H. (1961). *Art and industry: The principles of industrial design.* Indiana University Press.

Reinhold, L. (2008). *Modern jewellery design: Past and present.* Arnoldsche art publishers.

Simpson, R., Hughes, J., Slutskaya, N., & Balta, M. (2014). Sacrifice and distinction in dirty work: Men's construction of meaning in the butcher trade. *Work, Employment & Society, 28*(5), 754–770.

Watson, D. (2019). Fordism: A review essay. *Labor History, 60*(2), 144–159.

Webber, G., & Williams, C. (2008). Mothers in "good" and "bad" part-time jobs: Different problems, same results. *Gender & Society, 22*(6), 752–777.

Yeomans, R. (2005). Basic design and the pedagogy of Richard Hamilton. In M. Romans (Ed.), *Histories of art and design education: Collected essays* (pp. 195–210). Intellect Books.

Industrialisation of Animation Education

Michael Smith

Abstract This chapter explores the pressure on animation courses to produce highly skilled, technically proficient graduates who are 'ready for industry' and the pressure that this places on students to be technically excellent upon completion of their studies.

This presents a problem for academics, as there is only a finite amount of time to enable students to understand approaches to becoming a creative practitioner, develop a specialist practice and acquire practical, technical and effective communication skills. The emphasis that industry representatives place on purely technical skills presents issues for courses who are, at the same time, enabling students to become independent thinkers and innovators who can function creatively within their chosen discipline to a high level. The purpose of this chapter is to bring this discussion to the fore and explore the impact it has on students' approaches to their education.

Keywords Animation • Skill • Industry • Industrialisation • Students • Education

M. Smith (✉)
Leeds Arts University, Leeds, UK
e-mail: michael.smith@leeds-art.ac.uk

INTRODUCTION

The chapter will explore the current state of the animation industry and its requirements of its workforce, and how this has the potential to shape the future of courses, the ways that students think and approach their studies and ultimately, how they begin to think about themselves. The author has been working in higher education for over 25 years and teaching animation in some form for 15 years. These insights and an understanding of educational frameworks and government policy drivers together with the industry needs will form the basis of the chapter.

There is an increasing tension between education and industry as to what the latter thinks higher education should deliver to students. Organisations representing industry interests such as ScreenSkills (formerly Skillset) and Nesta (Hope & Livingstone, 2013) and industry leaders such as Tom Box of Blue Zoo have demanded that higher education does more to 'train' students to the level required. Tensions arise because training and education are different activities. Training involves teaching the individual to become competent and skilled at an individual task or set of processes. Education is a journey, an exploration of a subject, developing a deep understanding of a practice or area of specialist study (Coffield, 2008). Training can be part of education but not the whole.

This presents a problem for academics, as there is only a finite amount of time to enable students to understand approaches to becoming a creative practitioner, develop a specialist practice and acquire practical, technical and effective communication skills. The emphasis that industry commentators place on purely technical skills presents issues for courses which are trying to enable students to become independent thinkers and practitioners who can function creatively within their chosen discipline to a high level.

CURRENT ANIMATION INDUSTRY CONTEXT

Over the past few years there has been a resurgence and growth in the animation industry; this is in part due to the tax rebates that were introduced by the UK government putting the animation industry on the same footing as the UK Government Film Tax Relief (HMRC, 2016) that was previously introduced in 2006 (UK Finance Act, 2013). This has enabled film, television and animation to grow significantly in recent years and according to the British Film Institute's (BFI) Screen Business report of

2021 the Film, Television and Animation industry turned over £13.8 billion, contributing £6.1 billion to the gross value added of the UK economy (BFI, 2021). The 2021 report identified the growth in gross value added of the overall economic impact of screen related industries (direct, indirect, induced and spill over impacts) for 2016–2019 was £13.48 billion. Animation's direct contribution to this in 2019 was £285.2 million (BFI, 2021). Wells (2002) pointed out that animation also influences other forms of visual culture, such as feature length films, prime-time sitcoms, television and web cartoons, widening its potential cultural, social and economic impact.

The BFI expanded upon this by saying that animation alone generated £12.2 million in 2017–2019 through programming, merchandising, licencing and so on (BFI, 2021). As we can see the impact of animation goes beyond what we see on a screen. The ubiquity of animation has a significant impact; one example, Peppa Pig has been broadcast for over 17 years now and has just been recommissioned for another 104 episodes (Animation UK, 2021) which will no doubt generate a significant amount of money. Currently broadcast in 180 territories around the world, it has been translated into over 40 languages (Deadline 2021). This global reach is incredible considering that the broadcast comprises deceptively simple five-minute episodes about the adventures of a pig and her family. This demonstrates that the animation industry is a significant contributor to the UK economy.

The reports cited throughout this chapter identify research that has taken place in the animation industry and focus on animation production for children's television and animation for adults. It does not include the broader deployment and employment of animation roles within other related sectors such as Games, Visual Effects (VFX) or wider creative sectors. As such the figures of those working within animation is likely to be much higher with animation being heavily used in many feature films, games animations and other commercial applications.

According to the Inclusion and Diversity in the UK's 'VFX, Animation and Post-Production Sector' report (UK Screen Alliance, 2019) the animation industry workforce is highly educated with 93% having been educated to degree level and 23% of those also having postgraduate qualifications. The animation sector currently employs around 3000 full-time equivalent employees in the UK. Fifty-two per cent of the workforce are freelance, and approximately 25% are non-EU in the sector. The overriding reason cited for this is to draw upon skills that are not present in the

UK workforce. However, there are a number of voices from within the industry who are saying that despite being highly educated, they are not highly trained enough to meet the demands of the animation industry. Feedback from survey data in the 'We Need to Talk About Skills: A Skills Analysis of the UK Animation Industry' report states,

> Universities in the UK generally (but not always) do not teach or produce students with relevant animation skills or techniques to enter at an industry standard. More focus on animation principles and less on a full movie solely produced by an individual student means they could concentrate on better learning. TV animation is a team-based field and specific skill areas are required to fulfil [sic] each task. More joint projects from universities creating better quality productions and government led apprenticeships to help people ascertain the jobs that they want. (Animation UK 2018, p. 33)

Blair (1994) noted that animation is a multi-disciplinary practice, potentially drawing upon the practices of the cartoonist, illustrator, fine artist, screenwriter, musician, camera operator and motion picture director. It is simply impossible to give a student not only a deep academic, theoretical, conceptual and creative understanding but simultaneously to train that student to a level of technical excellence in a range of software within the timeframe of an undergraduate course. What often seems to be forgotten is that to be an animator requires drawing skills, an understanding of cinematography and film language, worldbuilding, scriptwriting and storytelling skills, acting and performance, sound design, crafting, modelmaking, software skills—and all of that before we can actually begin animating. We need to build these worlds and universes and then we can tell stories within them. Those worlds that are built are informed by a much greater lived or world experience which takes time to develop. Each of those areas mentioned arguably can be three years of study in themselves at undergraduate level. The skills problem is not restricted to the United Kingdom; recent research conducted for the Lithuanian Council for Culture: *Animation Industry's Expectations from Industry Specific Education* (Mitkus & Nedzinskaitė-Mitkė, 2017) has identified similar discussions between education and industry about the perceived issues.

> Evidence suggests that at this point there is a big gap between industry's expectations from graduates and what they can offer in reality. Academic institutions that train students to become future animation professionals

from the industry's point of view do not adequately prepare young special-ists to join the industry. (Mitkus & Nedzinskaitė-Mitkė, 2017, p. 286)

Despite the significant numbers of degree- and postgraduate-level quali-fied artists successfully working in the animation industry, there are those within the industry who are openly asserting that students are not prop-erly equipped to work within industry and that more must be done to train students in the right software. Training involves teaching the indi-vidual to become competent and skilled at an individual task or set of processes. Training is skills acquisition undertaken in a relatively short timeframe and then applied to a particular task. Education is a journey and exploration of a subject or specialist area to become informed and have a deep understanding of a practice or area of specialist study over a sustained period of time. Education is about a process of becoming (Biesta, 2017, 2020). Biesta (2010) has also described education as having three aspects to it:

- To become qualified in something, for example animation.
- To be socialised into a community, such as the animation industry.
- Subjectification, which is to be able to stand outside of accepted structures and formulate one's own opinion or perspective.

It is in the third element of education where critical thinking and inno-vation can be encouraged.

Training is a part of that educational engagement, not the whole and educators within higher education constantly tread a tightrope between academic, educational, entrepreneurial and creative needs with the require-ments from industry to have highly skilled, 'industry ready' graduates. Animation companies frequently have different workflows, use different software, in many instances bespoke or custom plugins and different set-ups. One could question if it is even feasible for undergraduate courses to educate and train students to the level of industry expectations, alongside the required academic discourse and other requirements as identified by the Quality Assurance Agency (QAA) in three years. According to the QAA Subject Benchmark Statements for Art & Design 2019, honours-level students should be able to demonstrate the ability to:

- Utilise subject-specific materials, media, techniques and tools with skill, understanding the professional, legal and ethical concerns of the subject.
- Bring to complex ideas, demonstrating, knowledge and understanding of their practice and contextualise this in relation to employability, enterprise, research, personal development and further study.
- Demonstrate an understanding of intellectual property in relation to their practice.
- Apply and extend their learning beyond their field of study.

Animation courses are finding it increasingly difficult to balance the tightrope and the demands from industry and organisations such as Creative Skillset and Nesta (Hope & Livingstone, 2013) are, at times, at odds with academia. In 2019, the UK Screen Alliance ran a series of 'crisis' workshops called Mend the Gap, industry liaison sessions that discussed employability issues within animation and VFX. The thrust of the discussions was that universities simply aren't doing enough to address some of those technical issues.

In the report 'We Need to Talk About Skills: A Skills Analysis of the UK Animation Industry' Kate O'Connor Executive Chair, Animation UK observes,

> It is vital that we develop a real partnership between the industry and education providers to ensure that our young skilled talent directly feeds into and supports the Animation sector in the UK. We have a significant challenge ahead, with a need for careers information and mentors through to developing higher level creative skills and talent and Animation UK will focus its effort on supporting the essential partnership and dialogue between the industry and education. (O'Connor, 2018, p. 1)

The question of who should bear the responsibility of training and ensuring students are ready for work has been raised in the past by former Vice Chancellor of Manchester Metropolitan University, John Brooks. Whilst Brooks' (2013) question is perhaps provocative, there is an expectation of industry that students are going to come out 'oven-ready' to be put into the white heat of the workplace. This is a difficult and unrealistic expectation when the industry and practice is so diverse. Whilst there is always an opportunity to develop and manage change within education and the industry, there needs to be much more dialogue taking place. Key industry players such as Tom Box (Blue Zoo) have said that higher education is not doing enough to 'train' students to the level required. Despite this rhetoric, Box (2018) asserts, "You simply cannot train someone to have five or ten years of production experience". It begs the question, are industry expectations of undergraduates simply too high?

Initial meetings between academics and industry representatives were insightful and there were lots of proposed actions to get academia more involved; however little seems to have come from it. Animation courses within the UK can do little to gain access to some of these organisations in order to have an ongoing dialogue with industry. Academics' only recourse is to have individual conversations with companies or on a small scale with industry attendees at conferences and festivals. The short-sightedness or unwillingness to have a more open dialogue is problematic; on the one hand universities are being told they are not doing enough to 'Mend the Gap' and on the other hand there is a way for higher education institutes to formally have a conversation with industry to attempt to resolve some of the concerns that the animation/VFX industry perceive that there are.

Another consideration that needs making is the breadth of application of animation skills to a whole host of other disciplines. Not every graduate will work in high-end film, television or VFX animation. There are many other applications where animation skills can be applied such as motion design, advertising, short form animation for the web, education, promoting social change and animation as an artform. The ubiquity of animation ensures that graduates of different levels of ability are equipped to work across a variety of industries, making work that has social, commercial and cultural value and not just a form of entertainment.

In light of the challenges faced by UK universities, that the aims and ambitions of an honours-level course are much greater than training alone, we need to take a much more flexible, more entrepreneurial approach to try to address some of the issues education and industry face. As Paul Ward (2019) suggests,

> Thinking in more depth about 'entrepreneurialism' challenges a simplistic binary: we either 'train' people to work in pre-existing roles in industry or we 'educate' them to be creative thinkers/makers. This leads to a bifurcation of 'skills' on the one hand and critical 'academic' outcomes on the other. Industry discourses about 'skills gaps', and universities' focus on employability statistics tend to further entrench this perception. It is

precisely because of this simplistic model, and the assumptions that underpin it, that we need more critical studies of specific approaches to animation education. (Ward in Robinson, 2019, no page number)

Jones et al. (2021) assert that within the higher education sector there are numerous challenges faced such as changes in financial, governmental and educational policies. However, universities need to move beyond the traditional remits of what they are known for and Jones et al. suggest,

> Within this context, a holistic approach (wider than teaching and research) is required by HEIs to address the building of innovation networks, create collaboration among HEI staff, students and businesses, and measure their success. (Jones et al., 2021, p. 5)

Whilst a holistic approach may be desirable, there are limits to what can be achieved within the scope of an undergraduate course. Some universities may choose to go down a more technically focussed route, whilst others opt for a much more creative and expressive path. Building networks and relationships with industry takes time and there could be limitations in terms of the levels of engagement to be had. It is the responsibility of a university to make their offer clear so that students can make an informed choice about the course they want to study.

UNDER PRESSURE

Student perceptions of higher education are shaped by what they hear and see on social media, and how courses are sold and promoted through marketing machines and careers advisors. Ashby-King and Anderson suggest,

> Higher education has been commodified as neoliberal ideology is reflected in and perpetuated through social discourses, such as memorable messages. These discourses socialize young adults to college and shape their understanding about the purpose of higher education. (Ashby-King & Anderson, 2021, abstract)

For some students, the sole purpose of going to university is to get a job and have a student experience that they have heard so much about (Williams, 2013). These memories and messages do not always acknowledge the demanding work and engagement that is required to realise what they wanted to learn when they joined a course. Parental pressure to achieve good grades and get a 2:1 classification or higher, then begin their careers straight from university is quite a heavy burden to be placed on the often still developing shoulders of an individual. In addition to this, students are often concerned with maximising and getting the most from their fees (Williams, 2013). In the paper, 'Exploring the Impact of Policy Changes on Students' Attitudes and Approaches to Learning in Higher Education', Tomlinson suggests,

> While students are concerned that institutions should enhance the value of the university experience in accordance with increased fees, they also feel it is up to them to 'get as much out' of the experience as they can and maximise whatever opportunities HEIs provide. (Tomlinson, 2014, p. 6)

The perception discussed here is that 'get as much out of' correlates to getting a good grade and not getting things 'wrong'. This binary of right and wrong, is counterproductive, especially in creative courses as it inhibits risk taking and experimentation (Orr & Schreeve, 2017). Fear of failure or disapproval from their tutors, parents or indeed their peers can be crippling for some. According to Judith Ponticell (2003, p. 7), "Fear of failure is the most significant negative emotion expressed because this emotion leads to more cautious behavior patterns".

Other pressures on students that need acknowledging are moving away from home, personal and social issues. Increasing incidence of mental health problems such as anxiety and depression are manifesting themselves within the student community. From a creative perspective and from my observations as an educator, students tend to judge themselves not only against their peers, but against what they see on social media, with artists presenting work with little to no context and produced with seeming ease. This apparent ease is likely to have resulted from years of hard work, creative practice or industry experience, and not from some superhuman ability. As Sennett (2009) asserts in his book *The Craftsman*, developing expertise and mastery of a skill or craft can take 10,000 hours of practice. This gives food for thought when an undergraduate qualification requires 6000 hours of study, especially as animation is a multi-disciplinary practice that draws upon many fields of study. Everyone has idols, heroes or role models that we look up to and aspire to be. However, students tend to forget that when they are watching the work of one of their idols, or the latest Pixar, Marvel, Disney film, or TV Series, there are literally hundreds if not thousands of person hours of time and potentially dozens or even hundreds of staff involved in such projects. Students measure up their abilities and therefore success/abilities against them and are often disappointed with their achievements. It's the equivalent of comparing apples to oranges. Students are not alone in the pursuit of perfection. In a trailer about his upcoming film Prologue veteran animator Richard Williams (1933–2019) said of his own career,

> I thought, I wonder if I'll ever get good enough to do this? it's something that nobody's just done, and something happened to me about three years ago. I know with all this teaching, all this experience is that, it's like yogurt it finally just went (squelch sound) and I am able to do exactly what I can think of. (Williams, 2015, no page number)

Adding to the self-imposed pressure, the vocal criticality of the animation industry about how universities are (or are not) educating students to the industry's required standards, does little for the students' self-esteem or confidence. It makes them constantly question if they are ever going to be good enough, have the right technical know-how, be skilled enough or even know the right software. The emphasis that students place on knowing software inside out is possibly misguided. Many universities teach fundamental principles and approaches to using software and there are many transferable skills that can be applied across platforms; the principles are the same, the buttons, or terms for processes may be slightly different. Also, every brief for a piece of animation will often present a different problem, lateral thinking and creative approaches to problem-solving are what are required.

We perhaps need to discuss further with students what constitutes success? Mitkus and Nedzinskaité-Mitké (2017, p. 284) raise the question, "Does it simply mean that now they (students) should be also commercially successful as well as artistically? But then can it be achieved without compromising the cultural value?"

CREATIVITY AT THE HEART OF ANIMATION EDUCATION

As with any arts-based practice, creativity is and should be at its core. Fundamentally animation is about storytelling and creative problem-solving through the medium of animation and moving image. "Animation can explain whatever the mind of man can conceive" (Walt Disney in

Thomas & Johnston, 1981, p. 13). This is a creative process and not just technically driven; it requires an understanding of the brief/problem being set, good research skills as well as practical and technical focus (Blair, 1994). Animation pedagogy is not just about filling students full of tutorials, or that idea of learning transfer and acquiring knowledge is about filling from one pot (the tutor/course) into another, and pouring information into students. Technical skills alone do not make graduates more employable. Perhaps we should think about the approach to teaching creatively focussed higher education courses such as animation as, "Learning as becoming, within a transitional process of boundary-crossing" (Hager & Hodkinson, 2009, p. 635).

So, the concept of developing an understanding of a discipline through a degree and then transitioning into industry, the 'boundary-crossing' is where we continue to learn. Perhaps the animation and VFX industry should see that degrees are a journey and a springboard from a focused area of study into a career, not solely a training ground and that we all continue learning; after all is this not one of the reasons many companies have continuing professional development programmes, or on the job training?

To be critical of all companies would be unfair, and there are some very good graduate training programmes which will take on individuals to help them gain a foothold in the industry. This is because they recognise the complexity of a creative education and that there is more to it that just training. The Head of talent at Framestore proposes,

> A creative education isn't simply about art, it is about learning to make mistakes, innovating, researching and coming to a fuller understanding of the world through capturing viewpoints and experience. (Smith in Haythornthwaite, 2019, no page number)

This is also echoed by Glen Keane talking about his experiences of working with Walt Stanchfield at Disney. Stanchfield said to Keane, "Don't be afraid to make a mistake. We all have 10,000 bad drawings in us so the sooner you get them out the better!" (Stanchfield, pg i, 2009).

However, despite there being some supporters of a flexible and creative education, there is such a dominant voice within the Animation and the VFX industry in particular, that there is the potential to railroad change through, that only satisfies the immediate needs of industry. If we are not careful and focus purely on technical aspects of these sectors, students will lose that ability to be creative and become those people who are very capable at procedurally pressing buttons in the right order. There is a place for people who are more technically orientated, who are more technically proficient, but this can be tailored though on the job training programmes via LinkedIn Learning or Pluralsight or organisations such as the AccessVFX. There are other opportunities to employ more technically minded worker such as, in the UK, apprenticeships, T-Level qualifications or bespoke training courses such as Escape Studios, FXPhd and Animation Mentor.

Undergraduate degrees should give students creative freedom, a space to explore, to find a voice and their own style. It feels like this is often forgotten by industry voices who've been through this educational experience. They want to fill the gaps that they have now without necessarily thinking about the future. As identified by Smith (2019) some of these broader, complex yet inherently transferrable skills are vital to a graduate not only gaining a place in employment but maintaining a career. One of the key areas that students need to develop in order to acquire these skills is to take risks, learn through testing, experimentation, possibly failure and importantly, reflect upon these experiences. This helps develop resilience, creativity and helps drive innovation. As Ken Robinson suggests, "The process of creativity can also be stifled by a sense that ideas unlikely to be taken seriously if they come from the wrong places" (Robinson, 2011, p. 237). Universities should be able to provide a safe, supportive environment where individuals can creatively flourish and develop, an understanding of their chosen practice over time.

CURRICULUM DEVELOPMENT

Institutions all have their own focus and agendas regarding curriculum development, all of which will give a course its own unique flavour or pedagogical approach to course delivery at the undergraduate level. As mentioned previously the QAA (2019) subject benchmark for Art and Design places emphases on employability, technical and specialist skillsets and group and teamwork as key attributes of undergraduate provision and learning.

The animation industry requires teamwork because of the complexity of the animation process. Pipelines and workflows are key to ensure that animation can be produced quickly, on budget and on time. A horizon scan of courses within the UK identifies that one of the key focuses of many undergraduate animation courses is the emphasis on developing technical and specialist skills within an animation pipeline, but from the evidence presented courses are still falling short of what is required. Many creative practices require teamwork or collaborative practice in order to maximise the full potential of a project.

Ken Robinson suggests that creativity does not arise only from an individual's performance but emerges from the interaction with ideas and actions of other people (Robinson, 2011). As individuals we engage with others, share experiences and relay stories and information to each other in order to develop knowledge and understanding of the world around us. Specialisation or rather exploring a specialist practice as part of a BA(Hons) Animation course allows students to develop a deeper understanding of an area of practice. Within the context of animation this means they could focus on working as a 2D animator, modelmaker, texture artist, VFX technician or one of the many roles in a production pipeline. There are numerous examples of this master/apprentice approach to learning today, particularly in craft-based practices that work well, but there should be more than one approach. One could assert that this is a sensible approach to developing skills knowledge and understanding that will enable a graduate to gain employment upon completion of their studies. Kennedy-Parr (2016) raises the question,

> Is this 'group work training' a short-sighted solution for today's industry creatives and directors to solve an immediate skills shortage rather than a longer-term solution for the durability of the British animation industry? (Kennedy-Parr, 2016, p. 92)

Kennedy-Parr asserts that students need a broader experience and that, "this creative freedom gives students the chance to find their own style, and voice" (Kennedy-Parr, 2016, p. 93). This approach, to find a style and to develop an individual voice is certainly one approach that can work very well for a number of students. However, one could question whether all students joining animation courses today want to become auteur animators or filmmakers at this stage in their lives. As educators, we need to acknowledge that the needs and skill sets that students bring to higher education have changed. We need to determine if the students' approach to learning has changed too. If we add the needs of industry to this equation we need to consider if our pedagogical approach to teaching needs to change too.

A balance needs to be struck that has a flexibility of provision and can accommodate a diverse range of practices. We need to devise curricula that encourage group work and sharing of ideas, develop and reinforce communication skills, negotiation skills, creative compromise and provide the space to express oneself. To do this and ensure that graduates are as prepared as possible within a three-year timeframe to progress into the animation industry with a portfolio of work that demonstrates the high-level competencies that are required by the industry is a challenge.

Moving Forward

This chapter does not claim, or attempt, to provide the answers to educators' dilemmas but rather to present the complexity of the situation.

Animation educators across the world are acutely aware that the creative industries require graduates to have a level of training and technical understanding. It needs to be recognised that this is not the sole responsibility of higher education, but potentially a mutual and collaborative effort between the animation industry and higher education. In order to do this, there needs to be an ongoing dialogue between both universities and industry. We need to sit down and engage in debate to discuss the differences between education and training and the pressures faced on both sides to ensure that between us, we can equip students to have a sustainable and productive career. We all need to acknowledge the broader remit of university education and where focussed industry-driven training courses are the best option. Within the United Kingdom the animation industry is represented by the UK Animation Alliance, which has an increasingly powerful voice in the promotion of animation and its requirements, but in order to support the industry it would be helpful for educators to have a seat at the table.

References

Animation UK. (2019). We need to talk about skills: A skills analysis of the UK Animation industry. https://www.ukscreenalliance.co.uk/news/animation-uk-we-need-to-talk-about-skills/

Animation UK. (2021). Peppa Pig finds new home with Studio Karrot. https://www.animationuk.org/news/peppa-pig-finds-new-home-with-animation-studio-karrot/. Accessed 13 Oct 2021.

Ashby-King, D., & Anderson, L. (2021). "It gives you a better chance of getting a good job": Memorable messages, anticipatory socialization, and first-year college students' understandings of the purpose of college. *Communication Education*. https://doi.org/10.1080/03634523.2021.1952462

BFI. (2018). Screen Business report (2018) https://www2.bfi.org.uk/sites/bfi.org.uk/files/downloads/screen-business-full-report-2018-10-08.pdf. Accessed 7 Nov 2021.

BFI. (2021). Screen Business: How screen sector tax reliefs power economic growth across the UK 2017–2019 https://www.bfi.org.uk/industry-data-insights/reports/uk-screen-sector-economy. Accessed 10 Feb 2022.

Biesta, G. (2010). *Good education in an age of measurement: Ethics, politics, democracy*. Paradigm Publ.

Biesta, G. (2017). What if? Art education beyond expression and creativity. In C. Naughton, G. Biesta, & D. R. Cole (Eds.), *Art, artists and pedagogy: Philosophy and the arts in education* (pp. 11–20). Routledge.

Biesta, G. (2020). *Letting art teach*. ArtEZ Press.

Blair, P. (1994). *Cartoon animation*. Walter Foster Publishing.

Box, T. (2018). *There's a problem and it's getting worse*. Future Publishing.

Coffield, F. (2008). *Just suppose teaching and learning became the first priority...* London: Learning and Skills Network.

Hager, P., & Hodkinson, P. (2009). Moving beyond the metaphor of transfer of learning. *British Educational Research Journal, 35*(4), 619–638.

Haythornthwaite, R. (2019). Creative industries urge the Government to recognise the value of creative education https://www.animationuk.org/news/creative-industries-urge-government-to-recognise-the-value-of-creative-education/. Accessed 11 Nov 2020.

HMRC. (2016). Television Production Company Manual. https://www.gov.uk/hmrc-internal-manuals/television-production-company-manual/tpc10010. Accessed 7 Feb 2022.

Hope, A. & Livingstone, I. (2013). Next Gen - Transforming the UK into the world's leading talent hub for the video games and visual effects industries. https://media.nesta.org.uk/documents/next_gen_wv.pdf. Accessed 9 Sept 2019.

Jones, P., Maas, G., Kraus, S., & Reason, L. L. (2021). An exploration of the role and contribution of entrepreneurship centres in UK higher education institutions. *Journal of Small Business and Enterprise Development, 28*(2), 205–228. https://doi.org/10.1108/JSBED-08-2018-0244

Kennedy-Parr, S. A. (2016). Does the current British higher education system really prepare graduate animation students for a developing and changing industry? *European Scientific Journal. Special Edition*, 92–99.

Mitkus, T., & Nedzinskaitė-Mitkė, V. (2017). Animation industry's expectations from industry-specific education: Lithuanian case. In *CONFIA 2017: 5th international conference on illustration and animation* (pp. 278–288). Instituto Politécnico do Càvado e do Ave.

O'Conner, K. (2018). We need to talk about skills: A skills analysis of the UK Animation industry, Animation UK. ANIMATION-UK-We-need-to-talk-about-Skills.pdf. Accessed 21 February 2022.

Orr, S., & Shreeve, A. (2017). *Art and design pedagogy in higher education: Knowledge, values and ambiguity in the creative curriculum.* Routledge.

Ponticell, J. A. (2003). Enhancers and inhibitors of teacher risk taking: A case study. *Peabody Journal of Education, 78*(3), 5–24.

QAA. Subject benchmark statement: Art & design. https://www.qaa.ac.uk/docs/qaa/subject-benchmark-statements/sbs-art-and-design-17.pdf?sfvrsn=71eef781_16. Accessed 3 Nov 2019.

Robinson, K. (2011). *Out of our minds. Learning to be creative* (2nd ed.). Capstone Publishing.

Robinson, A. (2019). *Educating animators academic conference 2019: Teaching the world's most expressive art form.* https://doi.org/10.13140/RG.2.2.30027.75048. Accessed 7 Nov 2020.

Sennett, R. (2009). *The craftsmen.* Penguin.

Stanchfield, W. (2009). *Drawn to life, 20 golden years of Disney master classes.* Focal Press, UK.

Thomas, F., & Johnston, O. (1981). *The illusion of life: Disney Animation.* Walt Disney Productions.

Tomlinson, M. (2014). *Exploring the impact of policy changes on students' attitudes and approaches to learning in higher education.* York: Higher Education Academy. https://www.heacademy.ac.uk/sites/default/files/resources/Exploring_the_impact_of_policy_changes_student_experience.pdf

UK Screen Alliance. (2019). Inclusion and diversity in UK visual effects, animation and post-production. https://www.UK-Screen-Alliance-Inclusion-Diversity-in-UK-VFX-Animation-and-Post-Production-2019.pdf. Accessed 2 Feb 2022

Wells, P. (2002). *Animation: Genre and authorship.* Wallflower Press.

Williams, J. (2013). *Consuming higher education: Why learning can't be bought.* Bloomsbury Academic.

Williams, R. (2015). Prologue 'trailer'. https://www.youtube.com/watch?v=G78qA9oreNE&t=2s. Accessed 30 Sept 2021

'How Do I feel About This?': Reflections on the Emotional Experience of Teaching in Art Education at a Time of Ecological Collapse

Eleanor Snare

Abstract In recent years arts universities have increasingly focused on producing 'successful' graduates through career-focused courses and employability initiatives which align with the UK government's economic priorities. What is this move towards industrialisation teaching arts graduates about their relationship to the planet? This research begins by identifying the industrialisation of arts education as symptomatic of the industrialisation of The Earth. It then proceeds to explore how scholars since the early 1990s have attempted to establish a new relationship between the two affected entities. Four positions gleaned from the literature are outlined: (1) anthropocentric, Eurocentric behaviour transmitted through art education; (2) communication of environmental crisis and ecological reconnection; (3) the de-centring of human perspectives and

E. Snare (✉)
Leeds Arts University, Leeds, UK
e-mail: eleanor.snare@leeds-art.ac.uk

S. Broadhead (ed.), *The Industrialisation of Arts Education*,
https://doi.org/10.1007/978-3-031-05017-6_6

99

(4) radical (de)instrumentalisation of art education. This research then takes a reflective, auto-ethnographic approach, analysing personal diary entries through the contextual lenses of these four positions and offering suggestions for how educators may attempt to navigate the intersection between arts education, industrialisation and environmental awareness in the future. It is intended as an introduction to the connections between art education, industry and The Earth, and the positions which art education does or could take as an influencer of cultural beliefs, emotion and values.

Keywords Anthropocene • Arts education • The Earth • Industrialisation • Environmental education

I open this chapter by acknowledging the unequal effects of the climate crisis on the human population: the deaths and destruction inflicted on those who have contributed least to the crisis, the citizens of the Global South and Indigenous peoples across the world. I acknowledge the systems of oppression which have comprehensively and adversely affected these peoples, and that I have benefited from these systems. I acknowledge my role in perpetuating climate crisis, and I acknowledge my responsibility as an educator to change this.

The ideas upon which this chapter is based were first shared during a symposium in March 2021, titled the Industrialisation of Arts Education. This chapter seeks to develop that initial research in a new direction by focusing more closely on the role of the educator at the intersection of arts education, industrialisation and The Earth. After a brief positioning of my experience, terms and research question, I introduce the theoretical context framing this work. Using an auto-ethnographic approach, I then examine a set of personal reflective diary entries from January to December 2021 through these theoretical lenses, and the emotional experience of playing a role in education at this time is brought to the surface. The chapter ends with some fuzzy generalisations (Bassey, 1999) for those in the art education institution.

Author

I have 10 years' experience teaching Fashion Marketing and Fashion Branding and Communication at undergraduate and postgraduate level in the UK, including as a module leader and in both red-brick universities and specialist arts institutions. The modules I have inherited and led during 2021 reflect the government-driven demand for industry focus in undergraduate education, articulated by the UK's Minister for Universities as "a focus on ... outcomes to fill our productivity gap, fuel our economy, and create opportunities" (Donelan, 2020). I led two 60 credit modules; one on digital branding and communication, the other on trend prediction and future careers. The curriculum is led by industry practices, and supported by theoretical and contextual learning which critiques these practices. Both modules include group work (un-assessed) and collaborative projects with other courses or colleagues overseas. All assessed outcomes are designed to be useful for students' development into industry professionals—for example, through creating a pitch document or professional presentation—while allowing enough scope for individual creative expression.

While government priorities may heavily influence this industry focus, factors external to the sector are also at play. Rosenthal (2003) suggests that the overwhelming nature of environmental, social and political crises has driven student desire for immediate gratification, expressing itself as grade-obsession and the need for vocational security, which then shapes the courses that are provided. There is also a practical need for industry-ready labourers in arts-based disciplines if its growth rate is to be maintained: in the nine years preceding 2020, the UK's creative industries grew at two and a half times the rate of the wider UK economy (CIC, 2020). However, in common with government priorities, all these are symptoms, not causes, of industry focus in education. The cause is the influence of the Industrial Growth Society (IGS), a term coined by Kvaløy (1974), which I will explore further in the next section.

Parallel to my teaching is my industry experience in branding and communications. I joined a national digital marketing agency as a content editor after graduation and worked with international fashion and lifestyle brands before moving to a communications and events agency, where I worked with large multinational companies on their internal communications. In 2015 I became a self-employed marketing consultant and began working with independent organisations and individuals in the creative industries. Over my career I have worked with approximately 60 organisations on their communications strategy, content and delivery.

I was working as part of the Industrial Growth Society, and specifically in marketing, whose sole purpose is to encourage consumption of goods, services and ideas. I was and am aware of its 'glamour': the spell it casts over our lived experience even when we are striving to extract ourselves from it. Part of this spell is the hedonic pleasure gained from experiencing or consuming material things; despite the long-term, widely acknowledged dissatisfaction materialism generates (Chancellor & Lyubomirsky, 2011), in the moment the interaction still feels pleasurable. Importantly, in my experience and taught discipline, the ability to cast a spell on others—to market, sell, brand and communicate to them so that *they* can experience hedonic pleasure—is also pleasurable, almost addictive. This personal history is at odds with my present, where the ecological consciousness that has expanded over my lifetime is now not so easily enchanted by the promise of these pleasures. My time in education has made me more experienced in the act of teaching itself while also pulling me further away, chronologically, practically and ideologically, from the very thing I am meant to be teaching. I therefore acutely feel the relational tension between arts education, industry and The Earth, and it is the navigation of this relationship which has pushed me to develop this research.

TERMS

In this research, 'arts education' refers to art and design education at undergraduate level in the UK; the location in which my own experience is grounded. 'Industry' and 'industrialisation' refer to organisations and institutions adhering to the paradigm promoted by the Industrial Growth Society (IGS). IGS has four features: continuous growth of outputs of industrial products (compared to necessities of life); output encouraged through competition; the use of applied science to turn humans and more-than-human life into industrial resources; and social fragmentation, standardisation and quantification (Kvaløy, 1974). Macy (2014) uses this term rather than capitalism as it can also apply to state-controlled economies. However, scholars use a range of other terms to refer to societies with these features, such as "consumerist culture" and a "techno-capitalist economy" (Anderson & Guyas, 2012, p. 226) or a "totalitarian consumerist regime" (Miles, 2016, p. 4). The Anthropocene—an unofficial term for our current geological epoch where human activity is having a measurable and significant impact on the planet—is part of contemporary environmental education literature but not without challenges. Neimanis et al. (2015) argue that the term does not reflect the unevenness of causes and effects of ecological collapse by and on different groups of humans, while jagodzinski (2018) suggests the term *does* assign specific responsibility to colonial, capitalist societies but highlights other terms scholars are using to reflect the specificity of the problem, such as Technocene or Capitalocene. I choose the term Industrial Growth Society because I perceive not only organisations but educational institutions display its four features, and in particular suffer from the idolisation of growth: the desire for more, for 'better', for infinite increase, without recognising that the world is finite and not a resource to simply fulfil our desires (Priestley et al., 2015).

I use the term 'The Earth' in this research to denote a singular, finite body in space and time *and* the rich, diverse experience of all ecological existences within and emerging from it. With it, I wish to give us a tangible reference point; something which inspires deeply felt emotions of awe or affinity to counter the alienation from the planet that may be experienced (Hollis, 1997), and which may still be felt with broader concepts like 'sustainability'. The Earth is a body, a place, a home; it is visible and present as part of our lives, although acknowledged to different degrees. This awareness of The Earth and our relationship with it is referred to as 'ecological consciousness' in this research.

QUESTION

The question I set out to explore is a reflective one: "What role do I play at the intersection of arts education, industrialisation and The Earth? How do I feel about this?"

I have begun to question the roles I have been enacting during my teaching career, becoming increasingly aware of a disconnection between the work I am doing, or am required to do, and the modes of behaviour I have outside of this job, and how these roles communicate or determine the way I am navigating the intersection of arts education, industry and The Earth. Identifying these roles helps me understand them as performances I step into at different times, or simultaneously, some of which are conscious and others unknown even to me.

The roles I am playing are complex: socially-determined yet with personal affinities, named and conscious or unconscious and nebulous. They are all acts of 'play': acts of performing and of enjoying the performance or of wrestling with the challenges the performance brings (in itself a stimulating game). For this research, I bring curiosity to the roles I enact and move between in my teaching practice, and the multiple different types of play I am taking part in at any one time. There are the roles I am consciously trying to enact as I bring ecological consciousness into my teaching; the roles I wish to play visibly, the roles I wish to be remembered for. There are the roles I am required to enact as part of my agreed fulfilment of the performance of a specific job title, and those which I perceive are required. Then there are roles I am unconsciously enacting which are part of myself: elements of my identity which become apparent as part of the 'play' only through reflection and self-awareness. Through this research I wish to tease out and name some of these roles to better understand the strategies I am using to navigate the intersection of arts education, industrialisation and The Earth. In this research I capitalise these roles to highlight their archetypal (or stereotypical) qualities.

In asking "How do I feel about this?", I intend to avoid the trap Sir Ken Robinson (2006) articulates: that as children go through school they are increasingly educated from the neck up with a focus on thinking rather than feeling. In the context of ecological crisis, in which grief, fear, anxiety and even the suppression of emotion are common reactions (Boeckel, 2009), it is crucial our embodied experience is addressed to be able to navigate this crisis, and to teach to and in that crisis. Inwood (2010) argues that art education, with its connections to the senses and emotions, can offer traditional environmental education powerful new approaches. Mirroring this opportunity, art educators navigating the intersection between practice, industry and ecological consciousness must therefore recognise the necessity of reintegrating our felt, sensed experience into the way we teach and the way in which we reflect on our teaching.

Context

The theoretical context for this research is significantly informed by David Orr's overarching strategy of teaching with 'earth in mind' to develop ecological consciousness among student cohorts. Orr argues "all education is environmental education … [that] by what is included or excluded, students are taught they are a part of or apart from the natural world" (2004, p. 12). By teaching with 'earth in mind' I seek to encourage behavioural changes in my students, and in the institution as a whole, to turn towards greater ecological consciousness. However, it is part of this research to reflect on the extent to which I maintain 'earth in mind'; what I am including or excluding as I design and deliver my teaching.

In a literature review into practitioner-led arts-based education for ecological consciousness, a range of strategies for teaching with 'earth in mind' were uncovered. This review focused on reflective, qualitative accounts from those practising the navigation of art education, industrialisation and ecological consciousness, and helped to determine the auto-ethnographic approach I have taken in this research which foregrounds the lived experience of practitioners.

From the literature, four non-chronological positions were identified, based on the phases in Ulbricht's personal account (1998). Position one in art education is the anthropocentric paradigm in which 'nature' is manipulated as material or subject within the art room without interrogation of the quality of relationship between manipulators and manipulated (Anderson & Guyas, 2012; Blandy et al., 1998; Blandy & Hoffman, 1993; Lankford, 1997; Neperud, 1997). Position two can be categorised by the development of specific pedagogical practices that communicate the human experience of the environmental crisis and/or The Earth's beauty while also intending to deepen and improve the relationship between art education and The Earth. Examples include place-based pedagogies that use cross-disciplinary approaches (Bequette, 2007; Gradle, 2007; Graham, 2007) and the development of an epistemological framework for Art Education for Sustainable Development (Illeris, 2012). Position three is the introduction of multiple voices into the relationship between art education and The Earth, including the de-centring of anthropomorphic perspectives through the application of critical animal studies (Kallio-Tavin, 2020) and biocentrism (Golańska & Kronenberg, 2020). Finally, position four argues for a radical (de)instrumentalising of art education to challenge anthropocentrism (Garoian, 2012) and encourage ecologically-focused beliefs and values (Anderson & Guyas, 2012). This position can be categorised by themes of parody, disruption and the reappropriation of industry mechanics (Mellor, 2015); educational spaces which encourage dissent (Gale, 2017) or responses to catastrophe, crisis and collapse (Gesturing Towards Decolonial Futures, 2020); and the de-instrumentalising of art education to be a non-productive event (jagodzinski, 2009). Positions two, three and four are illustrated in Fig. 6.1.

Fig. 6.1   Diagram of phases of eco-art education

MATERIAL + METHOD

The raw material for the analysis comes from my personal reflections. I have been keeping a daily journal since 2014 which has proved valuable in developing my emotional self-awareness. For this research, reflections were taken from a range of sources written in 2021: my daily personal journal, ad hoc reflections, those on my research process, and a weekly reflective diary on my teaching which I kept between January and May. One final entry was created specifically to reflect on the entire set of material and the research question.

Using diary entries which foreground emotion provides a specific fla-vour to self-reflection. Several scholars have taken an approach fore-grounding emotion and reflection when interrogating teaching practice, including emotion in relation to socially just teaching (Chubbuck & Zembylas, 2008), teacher training (Meanwell & Kleiner, 2014) and in understanding how emotional experience affects pedagogical strategy (Trigwell, 2012). Keeping consistent diary-like reflections is central to these methodologies, such as when Locke (2006) revisits journal entries made 25 years ago, in his first year of teaching. Bolin and Hoskings (2015) highlight that art education gives individual educators an autonomy unusual in other subjects, and therefore critical reflection on beliefs, actions and practice is essential to identify one's own purpose for teaching. If, as Burkitt (2014) suggests, even rational and critical reflective processes have emotion at the centre because our self is an emotional self, and our engagement with the world is inescapably emotional, then foregrounding emotion in analysis of personal reflections allows the reality of that emo-tional self to be seen, and to bring to light "hidden secrets that we all acknowledge" (Locke, 2006, p. 49). Reflection also provides a way to converse with a specific self, the role I am playing at that moment of writ-ing: "the image of our own self organised by our past activity" (Burkitt, 2014, p. 108) which may be very different to the image I am creating in *this* moment.

When considering outcomes from this arts-based research method, the importance of significance, validity and applicable generalisations that may be required for other situations or methods may not be relevant (Sinner et al., 2019). Instead, I seek to generate fuzzy generalisations which can determine what happened in my experience and therefore could happen elsewhere, suggesting claims for transferability that could be either possi-ble, likely or unlikely (Bassey, 1999).

ANALYSIS

Across the reflective material, one constant is the intensity of emotion I experience in enacting roles in my teaching practice. The reflective process offers a space for me to express and then consider these emotions; a space which may or may not be available to me when I am enacting the role of Senior Lecturer. Gilbert and Cox (2019) identify two responses to the climate crisis: a pulling back, retreating from the experience of living and being in our environment, or a reaching out, to build connections and

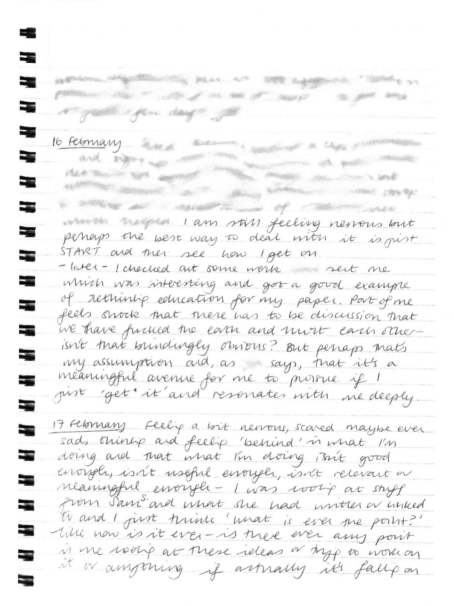

16 February

I am still feeling nervous but perhaps the best way to deal with it is just START and then see how I get on.
- later - I checked out some work ___ sent me which was interesting and got a good example of rethinking education for my paper. Part of me feels shock that there has to be discussion that we have fucked the earth and hurt each other — isn't that blindingly obvious? But perhaps that's my assumption and, as ___ says, that it's a meaningful avenue for me to pursue if I just 'get' it and resonates with me deeply.

17 February   Feeling a bit nervous, scared maybe even sad, thinking and feeling 'behind' in what I'm doing and that what I'm doing isn't good enough, isn't useful enough, isn't relevant or meaningful enough — I was looking at stuff from Sam's and what she had written or linked to and I just think 'what is ever the point?' Like how is it ever — is there ever any point in me looking at these ideas or trying to work on it or anything if actually it's falling on

Fig. 6.2   Reflective diary entry, 16 February 2021

relationships with The Earth and its species. I perceive my emotional response as part of the latter process: I am not pulling back from the lived experience of my roles, but neither am I reaching out (yet). I am emotionally recognising the reality of playing the role of Educator in a time of climate crisis, as indicated by the 'tipping point' in Fig. 6.2 where I realised "part of me feels shock that there has to be discussion that we have fucked the earth and hurt each other—isn't that blindingly obvious?" (16 February 2021).

This 'shock', of acknowledging the "actual lived experience" (Gilbert & Cox, 2019, p. 9) of not only me, but others unlike me, uncovered the psychic numbing I had been unconsciously enacting as a survival mechanism against the overwhelming experience of living through ecological collapse (Boeckel, 2009). This process of reducing emotional sensitivity when presented with events beyond our imagining may be, as Boeckel notes, essential for future survival. Educators must consider how to support students—and ourselves—in "participating in fear" (Boeckel, 2009, p. 11), as all of us experience ecological collapse simultaneously (although not in the same way). I play roles which contribute to that collapse— Consumer, for example—and yet also play the role of Senior Lecturer or Module Leader where I am required to mask the experience of both contributing to and fearing these environmental disasters so I can continue in the role without inhabiting the distress that can come with uncovering psychic numbing: "I realised how upset I was and cried about the futility of it all and even researching in this area when lives are at risk due to climate emergency" (17 February 2021; see Fig. 6.3).

An incident with a student highlights the need for these colliding roles to be acknowledged, as seen in Fig. 6.4: "I am learning how to maintain emotional security in my job, but it's also important for me to recognise I don't have to be 'strong' the whole time and can feel how I feel because it's real!" (22 March 2021). I am having an inescapable, embodied, emotional experience of my relationship to The Earth, even as I enact roles which ask me to put aside that experience.

I am also having an embodied experience of arts education. Anderson and Guyas suggest that because "art is not just an activity, it is an embodied way of doing and being that engages us fully" (2012, p. 238), it has a unique role in education for ecological consciousness. This complete engagement with art as an embodied practice is reflected in the personal values I bring to each role I enact within arts education as "my work and sense of self are intimately connected, no matter the strength of my

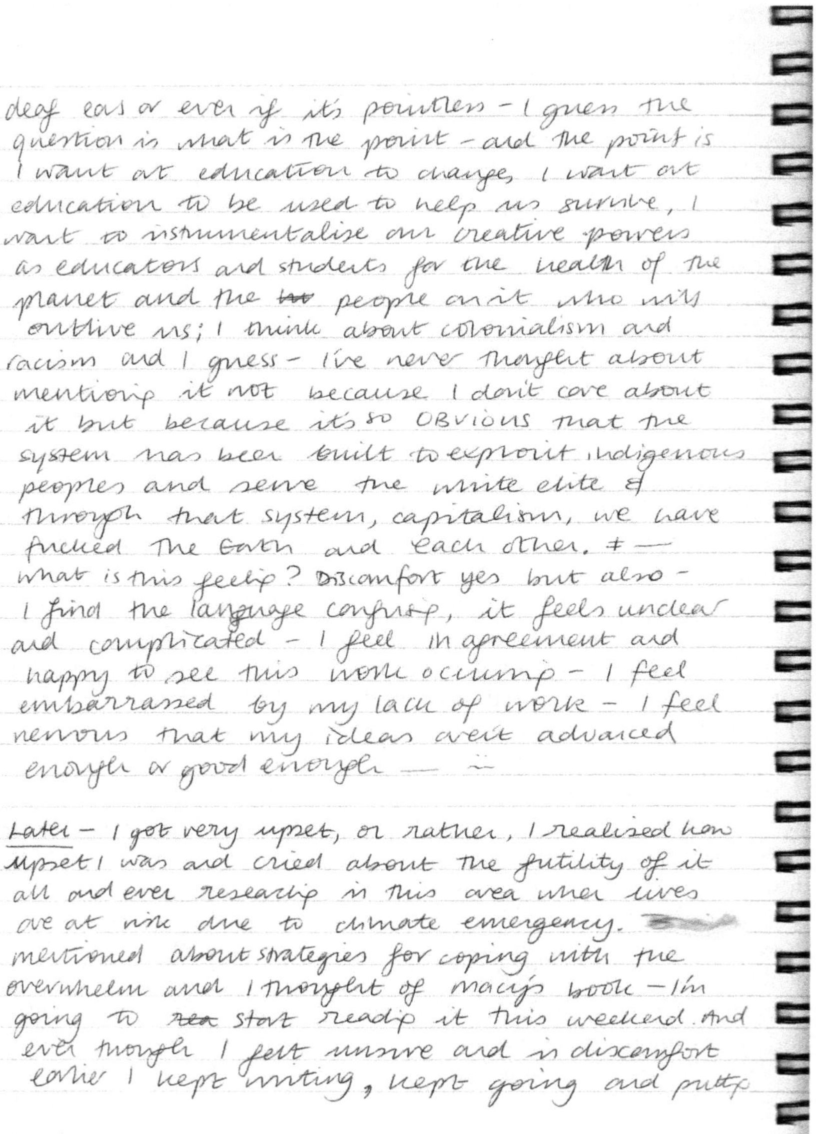

deaf ears or even if it's pointless - I guess the
question is what is the point - and the point is
I want art education to change, I want art
education to be used to help us survive, I
want to instrumentalise our creative powers
as educators and students for the health of the
planet and the ~~too~~ people on it who will
outlive us; I think about colonialism and
racism and I guess - I've never thought about
mentioning it not because I don't care about
it but because it's so OBVIOUS that the
system has been built to exploit indigenous
peoples and serve the white elite &
through that system, capitalism, we have
fucked the ~~Earth~~ and each other. + —
What is this feeling? Discomfort yes but also -
I find the language confusing, it feels unclear
and complicated - I feel in agreement and
happy to see this work occurring - I feel
embarrassed by my lack of work - I feel
nervous that my ideas aren't advanced
enough or good enough — ̈

Later — I got very upset, or rather, I realised how
upset I was and cried about the futility of it
all and even researching in this area when lives
are at risk due to climate emergency. ~~≈~~
mentioned about strategies for coping with the
overwhelm and I thought of macy's book - I'm
going to ~~rea~~ start reading it this weekend. And
even though I felt unsure and in discomfort
earlier I kept writing, kept going and putting

Fig. 6.3   Reflective diary entry, 17 February 2021

Fig. 6.4 Reflective diary entry, 22 March 2021

boundaries, and that in particular my values, politics, philosophies and spiritual beliefs are un-extricable from how + what I teach", documented in Fig. 6.5 (26 December 2021).

There is a desire for this *not* to be the case—that if I somehow just had stronger boundaries these elements of myself would not be entangled with my teaching role—and yet it is my lived experience. Hollis (1997) indicates it is a conscious choice whether or not art and its education is perceived as removed from, or integrated with, our lived experience and broader issues, and that teaching for ecological consciousness is predicated on this choice. Yet I do not know to what extent it *is* my choice, or I recognise it as a choice; it is instead a compulsion, an enacting of personal values or roles within the disguise of the Educator. For example, my emotional response to a curriculum critique was partly because my role as Eco-Warrior or Earth-Lover was under perceived threat, not my role as Senior Lecturer: "I had built it on my pedagogy and therefore felt invested in it. … I really care about … doing right by the students and future generations" (late May 2021), documented in Fig. 6.6. This 'nesting' of roles, of enacting personal values within a professional remit, is a theme throughout the latter part of my reflections as I recognise which roles I wish to

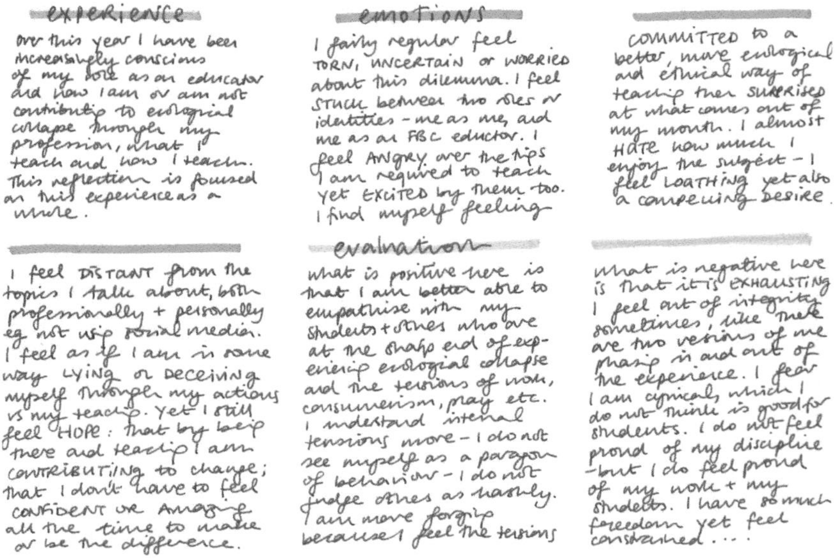

experience

over this year I have been increasingly conscious of my role as an educator and how I am or am not contributing to ecological collapse through my profession, what I teach and how I teach. This reflection is focused on this experience as a whole.

I feel DISTANT from the topics I talk about, both professionally + personally eg not use social media. I feel as if I am in some way LYING or DECEIVING myself through my actions vs my teaching. Yet I still feel HOPE: that by being there and teaching I am CONTRIBUTING to change; that I don't have to feel confident or amazing all the time to make or be the difference.

emotions

I fairly regular feel TORN, UNCERTAIN or WORRIED about this dilemma. I feel STUCK between two roles or identities - me as me, and me as an FBC educator. I feel ANGRY over the tips I am required to teach yet EXCITED by them too. I find myself feeling

evaluation

what is positive here is that I am better able to empathise with my students + others who are at the sharp end of experiencing ecological collapse and the tensions of work, consumerism, play etc. I understand internal tensions more - I do not see myself as a paragon of behaviour - I do not judge others as harshly. I am more forgiving because I feel the tensions

COMMITTED to a better, more ecological and ethical way of teaching then SURPRISED at what comes out of my mouth. I almost HATE how much I enjoy the subject - I feel LOATHING yet also a compelling desire.

what is negative here is that it is EXHAUSTING I feel out of integrity sometimes, like there are two versions of me phasing in and out of the experience. I fear I am cynical, which I do not think is good for students. I do not feel proud of my discipline - but I do feel proud of my work + my students. I have so much freedom yet feel constrained...

Fig. 6.5   Reflective diary entry, 26 December 2021

give voice to; which roles are best suited to answer a hearty 'Yes!' to Lankford's question "Do we ... believe that art education can and should play a role in the restoration and preservation of our planet?" (1997, p. 53).

The enacting of my personal values—including my belief in the power of art education—has overtaken my professional role, as "I have fallen out of love with my discipline but more in love with the role of 'educator' or even 'facilitator'" (26 December 2021). If I wish to shift my discipline and educational paradigm to one which has 'earth in mind', then letting go of "uncritical or seemingly 'value-free' curricular models" (Bertling & Moore, 2020, p. 60) is essential; so is letting go of roles which purport to be similarly 'value-free', or even ask me to act as if I am. I must keep "letting go of an old identity of being a teacher first and foremost, of defining myself by those terms" (9 December 2021; see Fig. 6.7), "LIVING WIDE OPEN" (8 December 2021) in my role as Educator if I am to teach with 'earth in mind' and fulfil Garoian's dream of contemporary art education as a method to develop ecological alliances, "becoming other and becoming sustainable" (2012, p. 298–9).

REFLECTION

What happened?
Emotions
Evaluation
Analysis
Insight
Behaviour

BEHAVIOURS (1) Remember that criticism is not personal; it is not ideological; everyone is a critic but few are gifted creators (2) Paint a picture of the vision before going into details (3) Ask for more specific help eg "I want to do X but I don't know how to do Y about it. What would you recommend?" (4) Remember you are great!!

Emotions I felt tired, frustrated, defensive and unsupported. I wanted to find solutions and co-creations but it felt difficult. I felt unsure of myself and the time I'd spent on the work. I am upset now because I feel I do not belong anymore.

Evaluation What was positive was helping me understand what to consider when designing curriculum. What was negative was I felt unsupported and even a bit embarrassed.

Analysis It unfolded as it did because (1) I had spent a bit of time on the work + therefore felt invested in it (2) I had built it on my pedagogy and therefore felt invested in it (3) I do not know some things about my role and feel embarrassed when I don't know them when I think I should know them (4) I work best when co-creating and/or being supported to achieve my vision rather than the vision being critiqued and all the holes pointed out (5) I want to be part of something and feel that I belong and my ideas belong but I need help to realise them and play to my strengths

Insight (1) I really care about teaching, pedagogy and innovation and doing right by the students and future generations (2) I need more help to get the details right / I need support with the details / I need to not do the details (3) I am emotionally invested in doing good work and struggle with unbalanced criticism (4) I don't do a good job of communicating the strength of my ideas which means I come across as not seeing the importance of details

Fig. 6.6 Reflective diary entry, late May 2021

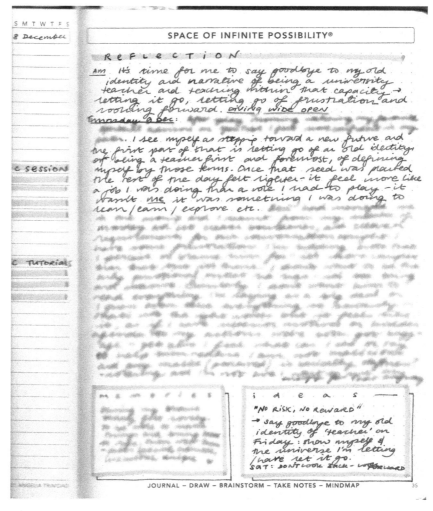

Fig. 6.7 Reflective diary entry, 9 December 2021

This dream, however, also requires the institutions of art education to choose this as their purpose. Cobb's critique of universities highlights the limitations of the current institution in engaging learners with 'earth in mind' while simultaneously recognising what *could* be done if the paradigm was shifted (2003). My reflection in Fig. 6.8, that the institution means "rules, regulations, security, safety, belonging … working together,

What does the institution mean to me? It means ... rules, regulations, security, safety, belonging, teamwork, vision — working together, mass impact. To benefit from the good parts of the institution I have to navigate the bad parts of the institution (imo). I have to work within confines to get the most impact. What if I can't do that? What if I'm too XYZ? (What if there is something wrong with me?) There are ways I fit into the institution & ways I don't - these are GOOD THINGS because it stops me from becoming what the institution can sometimes become: staid, safe, dull, set in its ways, redundant. LAU means [something] to me because its an institution I feel I can be part of without it making me less of who I am - I think it could make me more of who I am. I think LAU is an 'art school' in the way I believe in 'art school' — or that's how I perceive it, the lens I see it through. I see it as an opportunity. What opportunities am I most excited / scared of? Exactly the same ones: freedom, Responsibility, opportunity, support, Belief in Me. Leadership. I have complete opportunity to establish + drive my agenda, teach what, how I want, research what I want, support others, inspire others, push for a greater vision - and basically that's scary! Because I've said all my life I want XYZ and now I have it - how do I handle it? How do I make the most of it? WTF am I going to SAY?! !!

Fig. 6.8 Reflective diary entry, June 2021

mass impact" and "to benefit from the good parts of the institution I have to navigate the bad parts. ... I have to work within confines to get the most impact" (June 2021), echoes this critique.

For those at the intersection between arts education, industrialisation and The Earth, the institution can constrain or liberate pedagogical practice, depending on the extent to which that institution is still inhabiting position one, the anthropocentric and alienated paradigm. There is an opportunity to instrumentalise the communication of values and aesthetics through art education for wider ecological benefit (Ulbricht, 1998), and, being at this intersection, I feel strongly about this: "I want art education to be used to help us survive, I want to instrumentalise our creative powers as educators and students for the health of the planet and the people on it who will outlive us" (17 February 2021). In this ambition there is a 'nested' role: one of Change-Maker, someone who is going to revitalise the institution from the inside-out for the good of the world. Yet this instrumentalist approach may not be the most effective in navigating the intersection of arts education, industrialisation and The Earth. At this moment, everything is required to be productive, including art education, and survival depends on attaining a specific level of qualification (jagodzinski, 2009). If the Industrial Growth Society promotes infinite growth and the obsessive productivity that comes with it, then by turning the art school into another productive force—albeit for "the health of the planet"—am I simply replicating the myth that by doing *more* I will somehow 'solve' our problems of ecological collapse, when doing *less* might be better? Turning towards the non-productive is difficult for the Change-Maker, and for the institutional agenda. The UK's higher education is asked to focus on "outcomes to fill our productivity gap, fuel our economy, and create opportunities" (Donelan, 2020, no page number), while arts universities across the UK strive to turn their students into a productive labour force: from Arts University Bournemouth "turning creativity into careers" (2015, p. 1), UAL ensuring students are "well prepared for successful careers" (2015, p. 6), Nottingham Trent providing "industry-focused courses" (2020), to Leeds Arts University aiming for graduate success through "the delivery of an academic portfolio which meets market needs" (2014, p. 5). How might I navigate this "disturbing turn toward the professional" (Gilbert & Cox, 2019, p. 22) of art education without turning towards another sort of insistent productivity, that of 'solving' ecological collapse, and the sticky role-playing which may accompany it?

I may need to consider what the institution represents as I navigate this intersection, and what its reality may be. I write: "I think LAU [my workplace] is an 'art school' in the way I believe in [the] 'art school'" (June

2021). Yet Gale (2017) reflects that the conceptualisation of the art school which *I* believe in, a place of risk and rebellion, may no longer be available for this due to pressures and preferences for clarity and certainty from both institutional agendas and students. This tension between the art education institution which exists in my mind and personal history, and the one which exists now, in the minds of learners, has emotional repercussions as I navigate, and attempt to change, the relation between it and The Earth: "I am upset now because I feel I do not belong anywhere. ... I want to be part of something and feel ... my ideas belong but I need help to realise them" (late May 2021). Yet while I may find the current structure of arts education unsuitable, I still recognise the value of the institution, writing: "I see it as an opportunity" (June 2021).

This opportunity for the arts education institution is perhaps less about instrumentalising it and its residents to be a productive force, and more about changing our conceptualisation of the institution and the knowledge shared within. Gilbert and Cox describe the intention of their programme, the Land Arts of the American West, to "expand the territory of the university" (2019, p. 24) through a new curriculum grounded in the experience of those living in the region. While territorial expansion could be understood as colonial, it could also be read as a method by which the institution may generate a permeable membrane: an edge which meets the edges of the world and both become blurred. The knowledge shared within the institution becomes porous, moving from a standardised curriculum to one reflecting the lived experiences of learners and local communities—something identified as a key route into ecological consciousness (Inwood, 2008). This blurry, penetrable line is an opportunity to re-synthesise the fragmented, hyper-specialised knowledge which contemporary education promotes (Orr, 2004; Rosenthal, 2003) by showcasing interrelationships as crucial to ecological consciousness (Cobb, 2003) and, if not halting, then perhaps slowing, the dismantling of vernacular, local and indigenous knowledges (Orr, 2004). As an educator, especially one in a discipline asked to respond directly to the velocity of the Industrial Growth Society, I must be prepared for the sponge-like slowness this permeability may entail, and how I may need to enact a different role to move with it. As I note, "my tendency to reinvent the wheel (more exciting!) is perhaps getting in the way of creating a solid, repeatable piece of learning" (8 February 2021; see Fig. 6.9). My role is not to be an Entertainer, as can sometimes occur in creative teaching (Harvey & Harvey, 2013) but something else; to refrain from becoming "staid, safe, dull, set in [my] ways, redundant" (June) without succumbing to novelty or the thrill of directionless speed.

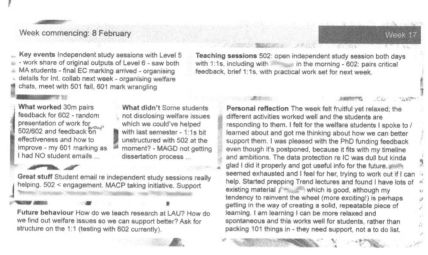

Fig. 6.9   Reflective diary entry, 8 February 2021

This permeability of the role of Educator asks me to question what I think that role is, what it entails and how it allows for myself to penetrate it (or not). My frustrations over enacting the role of Educator emerge, as documented in Fig. 6.10, when I recognise "i see teaching as something i love and am dedicated to, but i can't let it be my identity" because, in the context of navigating the intersection of arts education, industrialisation and The Earth, "I feel out of integrity sometimes … like there are two versions of me phasing in and out of the experience. … I find myself feeling COMMITTED to a better, more ecological and ethical way of teaching then SURPRISED at what comes out of my mouth" (26 December 2021). This is the experience of the "absurdity of the double life" (Norgaard, quoted in Illeris, 2012, p. 78); the recognition that ecological collapse is happening and yet continuing to operate as if it is not. It is characterised by silence and embarrassment (Illeris, 2012), stuck between two roles and somehow "LYING or DECEIVING myself through my actions vs my teaching" (26 December 2021). I know what I wish to do, and yet I do not do it, perhaps because I am "feeling rushed and pressed, like there 'wasn't enough' time" (9 November 2021; see Fig. 6.11). Is this in part because I do not know exactly what to do when it comes to arts education with 'earth in mind', nor have the resources to do it, as

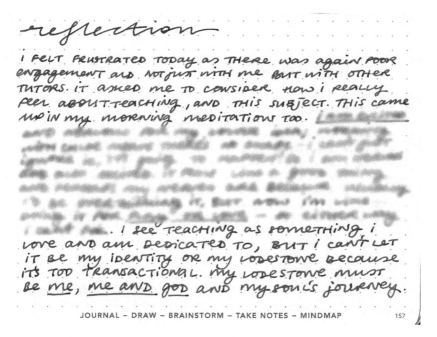

reflection

i FELT FRUSTRATED TODAY as THERE was again POOR engagement and not just with me but with other tutors. it asked me to consider how i really feel about teaching, and this subject. This came up in my morning meditation too.

...i see teaching as something i love and am dedicated to, but i can't let it be my identity or my lodestone because it's too transactional. my lodestone must be me, me and god and my soul's journey.

JOURNAL – DRAW – BRAINSTORM – TAKE NOTES – MINDMAP   157

Fig. 6.10 Reflective diary entry, 19 October 2021

suggested by Inwood (2005)? Is it because I am torn between training students for vocational security, helping them become competent in their discipline *and* instilling some awareness of the cultural responsibility which their degree confers upon them (Cobb, 2003)? Or is it because "I do not feel proud of my discipline" (26 December 2021) and its role in ecological collapse, so am uncertain how to weave it together with 'earth in mind'? There are no resolutions to these questions, only recognition of the complex, discomforting experience of navigating arts education, industrialisation and ecological consciousness.

Perhaps this is why, when confronted with the unpleasant tensions of the role of Educator at that intersection, my tendency is to seek something solid and affirming. I write: "[it] feels disappointing to put in a lot of work ... to not have [it] recognised. ... I'm trying to prove something" (8 December 2021). I agree with Denmead's position that, in art education, scholarship which has come before us must be remembered to prevent possessive and unnecessarily 'edgy' approaches (2020), yet it is clear I desire specific, individualised acknowledgement for the work I am doing:

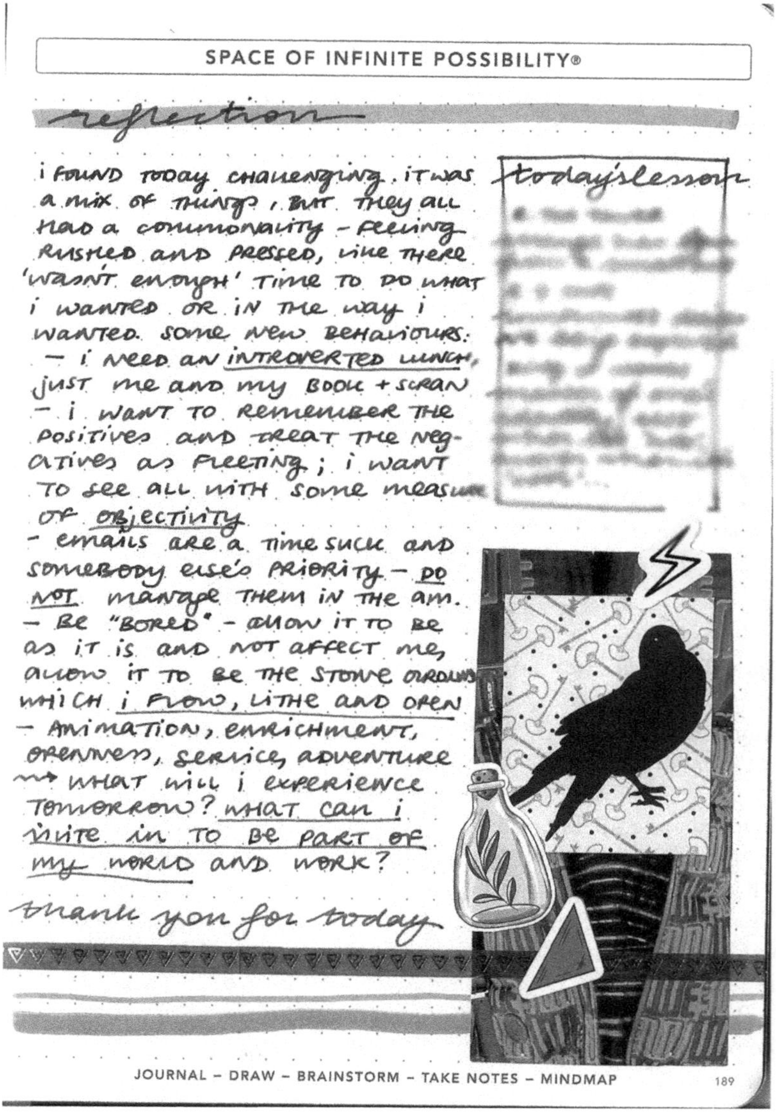

SPACE OF INFINITE POSSIBILITY®

reflection

i found today challenging. it was a mix of things, but they all had a commonality - feeling rushed and pressed, like there 'wasn't enough' time to do what i wanted or in the way i wanted. some new behaviours:
— i need an INTROVERTED lunch, just me and my book + scran
— i want to remember the positives and treat the negatives as fleeting; i want to see all with some measure of objectivity.
— emails are a time suck and somebody else's priority — DO NOT manage them in the am.
— be "bored" - allow it to be as it is and not affect me, allow it to be the stone around which i flow, lithe and open
— animation, enrichment, openness, service, adventure ~> what will i experience tomorrow? what can i invite in to be part of my world and work?

thank you for today

today's lesson

JOURNAL — DRAW — BRAINSTORM — TAKE NOTES — MINDMAP   189

Fig. 6.11   Reflective diary entry, 9 November 2021

"it's rare to get a well done or thankyou or good idea in the job I do" (8 December 2021). I also feel "embarrassed by my lack of work ... nervous that my ideas aren't advanced enough or good enough" (17 February 2021) when it comes to understanding ecological consciousness. This conceptualisation of my role as uniquely and unhappily *mine*, and the wish to receive special recognition for it, sits within the grand narrative of isolated and individualised egos that art education has constructed for its learners (Anderson & Guyas, 2012). Enacting the role of Module Leader, "I have complete opportunity to establish + drive my agenda, teach what + how I want" (June 2021) yet also feel "what I'm doing isn't good enough, isn't useful enough ... is there even any point in me looking at these ideas" (17 February 2021). By continuing to see my role as isolated from others enacting similar roles, and assuming that I have, if not full, then significant ownership of the educational experience, I am missing an opportunity to frame my role within the context of the ecological self (Anderson & Guyas, 2012), self-realised and supported through interdependence. Instead I am enacting the role of unacknowledged Hero or Champion, with the emotional martyrdom that accompanies this play.

My desire to be *recognised* for the work I am imperfectly doing at the intersection of arts education, industrialisation and The Earth is a desire to be successful in my chosen field and enact a role I will be remembered for. Yet this replicates the existing educational paradigm I have experienced which proposes education as a method of achieving success and social mobility which, in turn, generates negative ecological impacts (Orr, 2004). In trying to play the role of Hero I am instrumentalising myself for productive ends, but is that truly what is needed? A consistent theme through my reflections, unconscious in the lived moment, is that when I play an interdependent and porous role with students, I feel more fulfilled. When I played the role of "the water not the rock ... [I] remembered it wasn't all down to me to make it work for them" (11 November 2021); and that "I am learning I can be more relaxed and spontaneous [because] they need support, not a to do list" (8 February 2021). Despite the desire of students *for* the instructional to-do list and definite clarity (Gale, 2020), a co-created, interdependent curriculum with discussion about the needs of the cohort may be the first step for travelling the intersection of arts education, industrialisation and The Earth *together* (Ulbricht, 1998). This is a radical shift from my role as someone who has "been trying to solve the group's problems as my own, rather than letting them be navigated by all of us" (26 October 2021). Incessant problem-solving attempts may work, in the short-term, as a protective mechanism—for example, answering as many queries as possible "in preparation for Easter [break], mostly so I don't get shit about availability or have to answer email" (8 March 2021)—yet in the long term it only encourages me to play the role of Hero again, coming to their rescue and reinforcing our *in*-dependence. Instead, by continuing to sit awkwardly in *inter*dependence, "I am better able to empathise with my students [and] I do not see myself as a paragon of behaviour", to the extent that my role in the classroom significantly changes: "I have learnt I am less of a teacher + more of a student ... that I am learning how to /when to/if to teach 'earth in mind' as much as my students [are learning how to learn it]" (26 December 2021). I perceive that my individualistic success in enacting a role I have tried to play since the start of my career within arts education is less meaningful for The Earth than my potential interdependent enacting of those roles which it truly needs: "peacemakers, healers, restorers, storytellers, and lovers of every kind" (Orr, 2004, p. 12).

GENERALISATIONS

Offering fuzzy generalisations acknowledges what happened in my experience, and therefore may (or may not) happen elsewhere in either possible, likely or unlikely claims (Bassey, 1999).

First, it is possible other art educators concerned with The Earth are experiencing an intensity of emotion in enacting their roles. They may be working through, as I am, what their role entails and what they must let go of to be able to navigate the relationships between industry, art education and ecological consciousness. It is possible, too, that their conception of the institution is changing, whether tilting towards the instrumentalising art education for planetary needs, turning towards the non-productive or embracing ideas of a permeable institution which blurs edges with the world.

Second, it is likely art educators with increasing ecological consciousness are experiencing a form of psychic numbing or the discomfort of enacting multiple roles in tension with each other. There is likely to be a desire, or compulsion, to bring in ecological values to teaching, predicated on an existing embodied experience of art as a way of "doing and being that engages us fully" (Anderson & Guyas, 2012, p. 238). It is also likely these educators perceive institutions as either constraining or liberating their ambitions to include these values in their pedagogy.

Finally, the fuzzy generalisations I make as unlikely for others are not because I perceive myself as somehow more 'advanced', but because I am *not* advanced: I am firmly stuck in the tensions of the following realisations, a fish now aware of the water yet unsure how to evolve onto dry land. It is unlikely art educators are emerging from the grand narratives of isolated, individualistic roles which their own education has encouraged, and unlikely they are letting go (yet) of the self-instrumentalisation and accompanying martyrdom which is quickly achieved when working for a perceived 'greater good'. Interdependence, permeability of roles, co-creation and the sponge-like slowness which may be needed for effective navigation of arts education, industrialisation and ecological conscious-ness may feel unlikely or, at worst, unachievable within the current context of governmental priorities, job precarity, student desires and multiple, interlocking global crises.

CONCLUSION

The roles I play at the intersection of arts education, industrialisation and The Earth are roles in conflict, played competently and poorly, explicitly and invisibly, for my own individualistic success and the desire to be of service to students moving into an uncertain future. The discipline I teach, the ecologi-cal values I embody, the pedagogical strategies I use, my history and my present are all consistently in tension, reflecting the tension between compet-ing—and often un-articulated—priorities of art education, the Industrial Growth Society we are part of, and the 'silent partner' in the trio: The Earth. I feel frustration, upset, pride, fear, joy, embarrassment, disgust and complex combinations of these as I navigate these tensions, and these feelings do not go away when I walk into the classroom; rather, they are heightened. In offering this research and the fuzzy generalisations which conclude it, my hope is that some part of this experience resonates, and that through these potential commonalities we might form a more comradely path through the intersection of arts education, industrialisation and ecological consciousness.

In reflecting on this experience I am reminded of Gradle's words when writing about students engaging in acts of place-based creativity:

> each performer brings only the participation they can embody at the time, and takes away only what they recognize as valuable at that moment. The rest of the meanings, like so many of our endeavours in art and culture, are in storage for 'who we may yet be' to discover. (p. 407, 2007)

Perhaps the role I most keenly feel, and that which is most meaningful for me to play at *this* moment, in *this* intersection, is that of Learner: to be participating, embodying and endeavouring for reasons which, right now, I do not understand, yet trust their meaning will be discovered by the person I am yet to become.

References

Anderson, T., & Guyas, A. S. (2012). Earth education, interbeing, and deep ecology. *Studies in Art Education, 53*(3), 223–245.

Arts University Bournemouth. (2015). *Strategic Plan 2014–19* (PDF). Available at: https://webdocs.aub.ac.uk/Strategic%20Plan%202014%20-%202019.pdf. Accessed 13 Mar 2021.

Bassey, M. (1999). *Case study research in educational settings.* McGraw-Hill Education.

Bequette, J. W. (2007). Traditional arts knowledge, traditional ecological lore: The intersection of art education and environmental education. *Studies in Art Education, 48*(4), 360–374.

Bertling, J. G., & Moore, T. C. (2020). US art teacher education in the age of the anthropocene. *Studies in Art Education, 61*(1), 46–63.

Blandy, D., & Hoffman, E. (1993). Toward an art education of place. *Studies in Art Education, 35*(1), 22–33.

Blandy, D., Congdon, K. G., & Krug, D. H. (1998). Art, ecological restoration, and art education. *Studies in Art Education, 39*(3), 230–243.

Boeckel, J. (2009). Arts-based environmental education and the ecological crisis: Between opening the senses and coping with psychic numbing. In B. Drillsma-Milgrom & L. Kirstinä (Eds.), *Metamorphoses in children's literature and culture* (pp. 145–164). Enostone.

Bolin, P. E., & Hoskings, K. (2015). Reflecting on our beliefs and actions: Purposeful practice in art education. *Art Education, 68*(4), 40–47.

Burkitt, I. (2014). *Emotions and social relations.* Sage.

Chancellor, J., & Lyubomirsky, S. (2011). Happiness and thrift: When (spending) less is (hedonically) more. *Journal of Consumer Psychology, 21*(2), 131–138.

Chubbuck, S. M., & Zembylas, M. (2008). The emotional ambivalence of socially just teaching: A case study of a novice urban schoolteacher. *American Educational Research Journal, 45*(2), 274–318.

CIC. (2020). *Creative industries added £115bn of value in 2019.* Available at: https://thecreativeindustries.co.uk/uk-creative-overview/news-and-views/creative-industries-added-%C2%A31159bn-to-uk-in-2019. Accessed 18 Jan 2021.

Cobb, J. B., Jr. (2003). Can universities promote an ecological ethos? *The Structurist, 43*(44), 22–29.

Denmead, T. (2020). Forget this commentary too: Cultivating an antipossessive, nonessentialist, and anti-edgy approach to art education scholarship. *Studies in Art Education, 61*(4), 349–355.

Donelan, M. (2020). *Universities Minister speech at Festival of Higher Education.* Available at: https://www.gov.uk/government/speeches/universities-minister-speech-at-festival-of-higher-education. Accessed 18 Jan 2021.

Gale, C. (2017). #AlternativeArtschool //an interstitial space for creative dissent. *Art, Design & Communication in Higher Education, 16*(1), 99–114.

Gale, C. (2020). Art schools as a transformative locus for risk in an age of uncertainty. *Art, Design & Communication in Higher Education, 19*(1), 107–118.

Garoian, C. R. (2012). Sustaining sustainability: The pedagogical drift of art research and practice. *Studies in Art Education, 53*(4), 283–301.

Gesturing Towards Decolonial Futures. (2020). *Education 2048*. Available at: https://decolonialfutures.net/portfolio/education-2048-v2/. Accessed 21 Feb 2021.

Gilbert, B., & Cox, A. (2019). *Arts programming for the anthropocene: Art in community and environment*. Routledge.

Golańska, D., & Kronenberg, A. K. (2020). Creative practice for sustainability: A new materialist perspective on artivist production of eco-sensitive knowledges. *International Journal of Education Through Art, 16*(3), 303–318.

Gradle, S. (2007). Ecology of place: Art education in a relational world. *Studies in Art Education, 48*(4), 392–411.

Graham, M. A. (2007). Art ecology and art education: Locating art education in a critical place-based pedagogy. *Studies in Art Education, 48*(4), 375–391.

Harvey, B., & Harvey, J. (2013). *Creative teaching approaches in the lifelong learning sector*. Open University Press.

Hollis, C. L. (1997). On developing an art and ecology curriculum. *Art Education, 50*(6), 21–24.

Illeris, H. (2012). Nordic contemporary art education and the environment: Constructing an epistemological platform for Art Education for Sustainable Development (AESD). *Nordic Journal of Art and Research, 1*(2), 73–93.

Inwood, H. (2005). Investigating educators' attitudes towards eco-art education. *Canadian Review of Art Education, 32*. no page number given.

Inwood, H. (2008). Mapping eco-art education. *Canadian Review of Art Education, 35*, 57–72.

Inwood, H. (2010). Shades of green: Growing environmentalism through art education. *Art Education, 63*(6), 33–38.

jagodzinski, j. (2009). Beyond aesthetics: Returning force and truth to art and its education. *Studies in Art Education, 50*(4), 338–351.

jagodzinski, j. (2018). *Interrogating the anthropocene: Ecology, aesthetics, pedagogy, and the future in question*. Palgrave Macmillan.

Kallio-Tavin, M. (2020). Art education beyond anthropocentrism: The question of nonhuman animals in contemporary art and its education. *Studies in Art Education, 61*(4), 298–311.

Kvaløy, S. (1974). Ecophilosophy and ecopolitics: Thinking and acting in response to the threats of ecocatastrophe. *The North American Review, 259*(2), 16–28.

Lankford, E. L. (1997). Ecological stewardship in art education. *Art Education, 50*(6), 47–53.

Leeds Arts University. (2014). *2017–2023 Strategic Plan* (PDF). Available at: https://www.leeds-art.ac.uk/about-us/governance/the-universitys-strategic-plan/. Accessed 18 Jan 2021.

Locke, R. M. (2006). Teaching as an emotional experience. *Schools: Studies in Education, 3*(2), 31–50.

Macy, J., & Brown, M. (2014). *Coming back to life: The updated guide to the work that reconnects* (5th ed.). New Society Publishers.

Meanwell, E., & Kleiner, S. (2014). The emotional experience of first-time teaching: Reflections from graduate instructors, 1997–2006. *Teaching Sociology, 42*(1), 17–27.

Mellor, A. (2015). Professional parody: An examination of artist practices parodying and disrupting business models to new ends. *Organizational Aesthetics, 4*(1), 92–107.

Miles, M. (2016). Eco-aesthetic dimensions: Herbert Marcuse, ecology and art. *Cogent Arts & Humanities, 3*(1), 4–17.

Neimanis, A., Åsberg, C., & Hedrén, J. (2015). Four Problems, Four Directions for Environmental Humanities: Toward Critical Posthumanities for the Anthropocene. *Ethics and the Environment, 20*(1), 66–97.

Neperud, R. W. (1997). Art, ecology, and art education: Practices & linkages. *Art Education, 50*(6), 14–20.

Nottingham Trent University. (2020). *University reimagined.* Available at: https://www.ntu.ac.uk/about-us/university-reimagined. Accessed 13 Mar 2021.

Orr, D. (2004). *Earth in mind: On education, environment and the human prospect* (10th anniversary ed.). Island Press.

Priestley, M., Biesta, G., & Robinson, S. (2015). *Teacher agency: An ecological approach.* Bloomsbury Publishing.

Robinson, K. (2006). *Do schools kill creativity?.* Available at: https://www.ted.com/talks/sir_ken_robinson_do_schools_kill_creativity. Accessed 27 Dec 2021.

Rosenthal, A. T. (2003). Teaching systems thinking and practice through environmental art. *Ethics and the Environment, 8*(1), 152–168.

Sinner, A., Irwin, R., & Adams, J. (Eds.). (2019). *Provoking the field: International perspectives on visual arts PhDs in education.* Intellect Books.

Trigwell, K. (2012). Relations between teachers' emotions in teaching and their approaches to teaching in higher education. *Instructional Science, 40*(3), 607–621.

Ulbricht, J. (1998). Changing concepts of environmental art education: Toward a broader definition. *Art Education, 51*(6), 22–24 and 33–34.

University of the Arts London. (2015). *UAL Strategy 2015–22* (PDF). Available at: https://www.arts.ac.uk/about-ual/strategy-and-governance/strategy. Accessed 13 Mar 2021.

'Performance' Measures as Neoliberal Industrialisation of Higher Education: A Policy Archaeology of the Teaching Excellence Framework and Implications for the Marginalisation of Music Education

Jason Huxtable

Abstract Instrumental measures pledging to assess the 'quality' of education represent the latest turn in the unabating neoliberalisation of the UK education sector. As the proliferation of league tables, accountancy measures and 'common-sense' rhetoric around 'value for money' become normalised, the education sector continues to transform into a site of battle; a hierarchical competition of economic Darwinism. Higher education has not been immune to this seemingly irresistible cultural hegemony, embracing its own system of valuation, validation and competition through adoption of the Teaching Excellence Framework (TEF). Conducting a Policy Archaeology (Scheurich, 1994), I seek to show that the TEF embeds a

J. Huxtable (✉)
Leeds Arts University, Leeds, UK
e-mail: Jason.huxtable@leeds-art.ac.uk

© The Author(s), under exclusive license to Springer Nature Switzerland AG 2022
S. Broadhead (ed.), *The Industrialisation of Arts Education*,
https://doi.org/10.1007/978-3-031-05017-6_7

neoliberal governmentality, aimed at entrenching marketisation and industrialisation at the expense of teaching excellence. Through exploration of the policy's inception, the TEF can be viewed as an apparatus of industrialisation and represents one within a consort of educational policies which seek to devalue music education.

Keywords Music education • Teaching excellence framework • Policy Archaeology

INTRODUCTION

Music education in the United Kingdom continues to be subject to a process of systematic marginalisation and dismantlement. Despite valiant efforts by multiple stakeholders across all stages of state-funded education and schooling, the rationale for the continued support for music education in schools, colleges and higher education (HE) has weakened to the point of crisis. The constriction of musical activity in schools has not occurred through any significant change in the nature of music education itself however, but through transformation of how it is 'thought about' by a society who increasingly edifies and reinforces a grid of social regularities predicated upon the logic of neoliberal, capitalist and 'market-led' principles of value and worth. As education ceases to be visible as a social good, it's worth is subverted towards individualistic mechanistic transubstantiations of private cultural capital towards private economic gain, functioning as 'meritocratic' apparatus for widening inequality and class divide. As a music educator with experience at all stages of the UK state sector, I have experienced the disquieting emotions of the continual 'turning of the screw' against mobilisation of the powerful personal, social and critical transformations I know music education can catalyse. Further investigation of the forces operating within this ideological fixation and the processes towards contemporary rationale is necessary to both understand the basis for this anxiety but also to strategise opposition and, more positively, the imagination of utopian futures.

My agency and activity as a music educator is currently, predominantly, within higher education and, consequently, I am interested in the investigating the policy landscape which contextualises 'common-sense' decision making at this level and the implications for music and its sustainability. How, for example, is higher music education affected by 'industrial' visions of educational functionality and, more importantly, to what extent is complicit policy enaction reinforcing similar ideological rationale? What is the future for higher education music in the UK and to what extent is self-strangulation inevitable through higher education's adoption of neoliber-alising, industrial, processes of policy formation; policy ideologically infused with that already proving disastrous for UK schools? In this study I aim to conduct a policy analysis of the Teaching Education Framework using a Policy Archaeology methodology. This methodology examines the social regularities which allow specific policy problems and solutions to come into view and reveals the ideological contexts for this fixing of socially regulated 'governmentality'. I hope to reveal the conditions for the policy adoption of the Teaching Excellence Framework (TEF) and the possible implications for the future marginalisation of music education.

THE TEACHING EXCELLENCE FRAMEWORK

The Teaching Excellence Framework has become an accepted system of seemingly objective measurement of teaching quality within the UK Higher Education (HE) sector. Since its inception, it has functioned as a driver of rapid sectoral change, impacting significantly upon stakeholders. First introduced within the Department for Business, Innovation and Skills' Green Paper (BIS, 2015), the TEF constitutes an important aspect of the subsequent 'policy ensemble' (DfE, 2016; BIS, 2016a, b), culminating in the Higher Education Research Act (2017).

The TEF awards higher education providers with a Bronze, Silver or Gold rating based on their performance against benchmarked metrics. A range of data sources are used as proxy measures to ascertain student's assessment of 'the teaching on my course' 'assessment and feedback', and the 'academic support' they receive. 'Continuation' rates, levels of 'employment or further study' and graduate's securing of 'highly skilled employment or further study' are combined with provider statements to form a judgement on the quality of teaching at registered institutions.

Primarily concerned with ensuring 'clear incentives for higher education institutions to deliver value to students and taxpayers' (BIS, 2016b), the TEF rewards 'successful' institutions with 'reputational and financial incentives' (BIS, 2015). Although the framework's aim, benevolent as it would appear, is to promote and reward teaching excellence, the TEF caused controversy across the sector at inception with significant concerns raised relating to its ability to deliver positive outcomes.

A range of critical perspectives were voiced through this process of policy formation and adoption. One can only measure what is defined, with 'Teaching Excellence' representing a repeatably contested term requiring further research and definition (Ashwin, 2017). One study, aiming to uncover consensus, found that most participants involved found it impossible to measure teaching excellence, undermining the central premise of the framework (Wood & Su, 2017). Use of proxy measures within the TEF also attracted criticism with the supposed correlation between student satisfaction and teaching quality particularly contestable (Gunn, 2018), measuring the wrong things (Race, 2017). Most damning is where the TEF was viewed as a negative pedagogic force, poised to reduce standards due to cost pressures (Barkas et al., 2017), constituting a policy mechanism for surveillance and control (Heaney & Mackenzie, 2017). The conclusion from sector groups was that 'there are genuine concerns about how the assessment defines and measures teaching excellence' (Universities UK 2017, p. 2). Student groups also agreed that the TEF was unlikely to improve teaching quality (Oxford Student Union, BIS, 2016a).

With such widespread condemnation at both consultative stage and in implementation, it seems necessary to ask; how did the TEF come to be implemented and under what social conditions? What are the ideological underpinnings of this policy, what are the potential harms and are there parallels across the wider UK education sector which could be made?

POLICY ARCHAEOLOGY: DIGGING FOR 'SOCIAL REGULARITIES'

Policy Archaeology was introduced by James Scheurich as a 'radically different approach to policy studies in education' (Scheurich, 1994, p. 297). Scheurich aims to reconceptualise policy studies to be primarily concerned with, and framed by, the 'social construction' of policy problems/solutions, asking how a 'grid of social regularities' interact with policy action, reaction and enaction. Policy Archaeology offers a highly appropriate methodological framework to examine the conditions (societal, political and ideological) that brought about the application of the TEF as an 'acceptable', although not widely merited, means of measuring Teaching Excellence and Student Outcomes within the UK Higher Education sector.

Policy Archaeology has not been widely employed as a methodological tool for policy analysis. However, it has found some utility by policy analysts, particularly in relation to the social regularities that contextualise policy relating to bullying in schools. Bailey (2017) and Walton (2010) both use Policy Archaeology to uncover ways of understanding ideological and cultural aspects of bullying policy in relation to their own grid of social regularities (Walton, 2010), for example how policy interacts with Catholic ideology within Irish schools (Bailey, 2017). Policy Archaeology has also been considered in comparison to other existing methods of policy analysis (Gale, 2001).

Policy Archaeology of the social construction of problems, and associated policy solutions, challenges the policy analyst to identify the 'constitutive grid of conditions, assumptions, forces which make the emergence of a social problem' possible and 'to investigate how a social problem becomes visible as a social problem' (Scheurich, 1994, p. 300). More radically, policy analysts are required to examine policy studies itself, reflecting on the nature of how these constitutive grid of conditions influence, and are embedded within, the wider theoretical discipline and within the individual analyst. Through the counting, labelling and description of problems and problem groups, policy analysts are 'key in the construction of such problems and groups and … legitimize these constructions' (Scheurich, 1994, p. 311). Policy archaeologists are concerned with uncovering how policy problems and possible solutions come into view, predicated on the fundamental tenet that only 'acceptable' solutions can be adopted by a society viewing themselves, and their problems, through a particular socio-economic-political-historical lens; what exists as viewable inside the 'overton window' as acceptable, 'sensible' and politically available policy solutions.

Policy Archaeology provides a framework for examining policy and associated issues of 'social construction' through the transitional 'passing' through of four arenas. The four arenas act as particular lenses to view both the policy and the constitutive grid of regularities, encouraging analysts to move around these arenas until new insights are exhausted. The arenas, whilst distinct, are semi-permeable and Scheurich recognises overlaps and shared aspects. In brief, the four arenas explore: (1) The study of the social construction of social problems, (2) The identification of the network of social regularities that contextualise problems, (3) The study of the social construction of the range of acceptable policy solutions and (4) The study of the social functions of policy studies itself (Scheurich, 1994).

What are the social problems which the TEF seeks to 'solve' and what constitutes the grid of social regularities which the TEF exists within and therefore mirrors?

Through the passing of the policy through these arenas, primarily 2 and 3, I seek to uncover and reveal the social regularities the TEF exists within and how these manifest within the policy. How does the policy explicitly reflect, and reinforce, this grid of social regularities and how can conclusions lead towards a praxis based (Freire, 1972) response for change? To what extent is there potential to alter what may be 'viewable' as problems and solutions into the future?

The Grid of Social Regularities (Arena 2)

Scheurich, in relation to his case study applying Policy Archaeology to school services for 'previously ignored' groups, identifies five social regularities, categories which can form a language to describe social interaction, forms of 'Capital' and acceptable/unacceptable interactions between social agents ('gender, race, class, governmentality and professionalization'). One of these regularities is 'Governmentality', a 'kind of governance that counts, describes, defines, that brings everything under its gaze' (Scheurich, 1994, p. 306), a kind of governmental rationality that equates well-being to that which can be counted (Scheurich, 1994). This definition of Governmentality is underpinned by his belief of the larger liberal world view, collectively assuming that free enterprise economies are the best (Scheurich, 1994).

'Freedom of enterprise' and 'market freedom' relate to Neoliberal ideology, linked to governmentality by Foucault (Lemke, 2001) in his lecture at the Collège de France. The link between neoliberalism, regulation and governmentality has also been made by multiple commentators (e.g. Olssen & Peters, 2005) and has become central to discourse of and from the sector. The literature widely supports the view that the nature of HE governance and policy activity reflects the domination of Neoliberal ideology, supporting Scheurich's view of liberal governmentality representing an important, and legitimate, aspect of the 'grid of social regularities' to be examined. Discursive activity linking higher education to Neoliberalism is, therefore, important in understanding the social regularities HE, and HE policy exist within.

Neoliberalisation and Higher Education

Neoliberalism has been defined in many overlapping ways, primarily highlighting the centrality of 'The Market' to act as a mechanism for competition, individuality and as solution to social problems in the best interests of society's individuals. Bhopal's (2018) selected definition illustrates explicitly the relationship between policy and ideology; policy not just of neoliberalism but AS neoliberalism.

Neoliberalism has been defined as:

> *an ensemble of economic and social policies, forms of governance, and discourses and ideologies that promote individual self-interest, unrestricted flows of capital, deep reductions in the cost of labour and sharp retrenchment of the public sphere. Neoliberals champion privatisation of social goods and withdrawal of government from provision for social welfare on the premise that competitive markets are more effective and efficient.* (Bhopal, 2018, p. 2)

This definition links policy ensembles (TEF) with forms of governance (governmentality), ideologies (neoliberalism) and discourses (literature on neoliberalism in HE) forming a convincing platform to explore the grid of regularities as applied to the TEF. It is also interesting to note the synergetic intersectionality between neoliberalism and racial inequality which both Scheurich, in his case study highlighting mutations of White Supremacy, and Bhopal identify; this definition is positioned at the very beginning of 'White Privilege: The Myth of a Post-Racial Society' (Bhopal, 2018)!

Within 'How we got here: UK higher education under neoliberalism', Radice states that neoliberalism remains the dominant political philosophy across the world and its utility 'stems from the multiple key functions of HE within capitalism' such as 'providing higher level work skills' (Radice, 2013). 'There is a common set of assumptions and practices driving the transformation of higher education into an adjunct of corporate power and values' (Giroux, 2014) with the sector reaching a point of deep neoliberal entrenchment ceaselessly framed by the logic of marketisation (Canaan, 2013). This marketisation is viewable from multiple angles such as the adoption of principles of marketing principles (Askehave, 2007) and customer survey analysis (Lucas, 2018), importing the strategies and methods of private business to public institutions (Connell, 2013), exemplifying a new capitalist state formation (Ainley, 2004).

Discourse has also altered to mirror this institutional shift, reinforcing and making real this new 'reality'. The overwhelming weight of discourse relating to the marketisation within HE is convincing, the marketisation of higher education is linked to neoliberal capitalism (Cruickshank, 2016) with successive government policy discourses moving to emphasise only the economic role of HE (Barkas et al., 2017), framing Universities as competing businesses selling products in the free market to student customers (Fairclough, 1993). Similar themes of discourse also emerge from within the institution with academic leaders mirroring, echoing and reinforcing neoliberal and neoliberalising market-based logic (Mautner, 2005). 'The Assault on Universities' comes from all angles, resulting in the UK's Higher Education sector transforming 'into a patchwork of academic supermarkets' (Freedman, 2011).

The TEF has also been directly linked to this predominantly neoliberalist, marketising agenda in transformation of the wider HE sector (Barkas et al., 2017). Not only linked to neoliberalist ideology, some commentators highlight the central role TEF plays in depicting neoliberal transformation, with the TEF playing an 'important role in neoliberal interventionism in English higher education' (Cruickshank, 2016). Gunn identifies the TEF as the framework of the neoliberal market (Gunn, 2018) with its implementation subjecting HE to further 'processes of neoliberalisation, management, control, supervision, metricisation, marketisation, casualisation and precarisation' (Heaney & Mackenzie, 2017, no page no). Quite clearly, HE is in the grip of neoliberal ideology with TEF central to, and a continuation of, this condition. However, how does the TEF, specifically, embed neoliberal ideology and where can this be identified within the wider policy ensemble?

How Does TEF Function an Instrument of Neoliberalism? Policy Analysis

Neoliberalism seeks to establish 'the proper functioning of markets. Furthermore, if markets do not exist (in areas such as land, water, *education*, health care, social security or environmental pollution) then they must be created' (Harvey, 2005, p. 2). The creation of market driven systems is central to the neoliberal project. In fact, 'Neoliberals have had astonishing success in creating markets for things whose commodification was once almost unimaginable' (Connell, 2013, p. 100). How does the

TEF aim to create a market, and in doing so, reflect neoliberal ideology and the associated grid of social regularities?

There are many definitions of what a market is, its features and characteristics (e.g. Business Dictionary (2018), The Balance (2018), Important India (2016)). Although exact terms vary slightly, definitions identify and coalesce around shared themes of how a healthy market operates:

- Creates systems of differential pricing to distinguish products.
- Promotes competition between producers.
- Uses regulatory bodies to oversee fairness within the market.

Extracting indicative text from 'Success as a Knowledge Economy: Teaching Excellence, Social Mobility and Student Choice' (BiS, 2016b) white paper, a policy document fundamental to the implementation of the TEF, I will illustrate how characteristics of the market are proposed. I will also then identify how these characteristics are also referenced within the wider literature, suggesting the 'effect' of the policy.

Differential Pricing

Problem:

We need action to address the ... variation in quality and outcomes experience by some students. (p. 5)

Courses are inflexible, based on the traditional three-year undergraduate model, with insufficient innovation and provision of two-year degrees and degree apprenticeships. (p. 8)

Solution:

TEF is intended to generate reputational as well as financial incentives. The reputational advantage that will accrue to providers achieving the highest TEF ratings will be substantial. ... But we think that teaching excellence should be recognised by providing for the best providers to maintain their tuition fees in line with inflation. (p. 49)

New and innovative providers offering high quality higher education continue to face significant and disproportionate challenges to establishing themselves in the sector. Making it easier for these providers to enter and expand will help drive up teaching standards overall. (p. 9)

In effect:

Differential pricing will be introduced through the ability for the 'best providers' to raise their fees in line with inflation. Less successful providers will, consequently, be required to reduce their fees in real terms. This will have the effect of producing a market with products sold at different 'prices', reflecting the 'quality' and prestige of competing products. New providers will be able to charge significantly lower fees through accelerated degree programmes and two-year degrees, effectively slashing the overall 'investment', and debt accrued, of a degree programme.

Commodification of higher education begun during the Thatcher government through significant cuts in HE (Wilby, 2013) resulting in a necessity for international students to be charged tuition fees, creating the ideological conditions for HE to be bought and sold like a market product (Canaan, 2013). Subsequent increases in tuition fees have been linked to funding deficits and requirement to lighten the burden on the tax payer (IFS, 2011). Most recently, the use of the National Student Survey, central to institution's TEF success (Gillard, 2018), is being used as a proxy from price mechanism (Cruickshank, 2016) with the TEF presented as an instrumental mechanism linked to tuition fee rises (Gillard, 2018). Through this function it helps to objectify price mechanism, solving the negative political implications of 'direct' government intervention (Gunn, 2018).

Promoting Competition

Problem:

there is more to be done for our university system to fulfil its potential as an engine of social mobility.

Many students are dissatisfied with the provision they receive.

Employers are suffering skills shortages.

Courses are inflexible.

At the heart of this lies insufficient competition and a lack of informed choice. (p. 7–8)

Solution:

Competition between providers in any market incentivises them to raise their game, offering consumers a greater choice of more innovative and better-quality products and services at lower cost. Higher education is no exception. (p. 8)

Universities *'create the knowledge, capability and expertise that drive competitiveness and nurture the values that sustain our open democracy' (p. 5)*

We will make it quicker and easier for new high quality challenger institutions to enter the market and award their own degrees. (p. 6)

There is no compelling reason for incumbents to be protected from high quality competition. We want a globally competitive market that supports diversity. (p. 8)

Making it easier for these providers to enter and expand will help drive up teaching standards overall; enhance the life chances of students; drive economic growth; and be a catalyst for social mobility. (p. 9)

By introducing more competition and informed choice into higher education, we will deliver better outcomes and value for students, employers and the taxpayers who underwrite the system. (p. 8)

In effect:

'Rewarding excellence breeds competition' (Race, 2017); the nature of excellence defines that not everything can be so. Through the creation of hierarchising systems and the rationing of the 'best', gold standard products, the TEF effectively introduces competitive market structures (Connell, 2013). Heaney & Mackenzie (2017, no page number) conclude that and the white paper, 'reifies, glorifies and fetishises competition and marketisation'.

The notion that increased competition will act as an 'engine of social mobility' is at odds with Ainley's view that competition within the 'market-state' has increased division in society with inequality widening as a result of neoliberal marketisation (Ainley, 2004). Within these conditions, and as HEIs look to corporate programmes to develop their competitive edge (Askehave, 2007) through adoption of corporate practices and business models (Barkas et al., 2017), more competition is likely to reduce the quality of teaching and research capacity and autonomy.

Use of Regulatory Bodies

Problem:

HEFCE's purpose, role and powers have become outdated. (p. 15)

As recognised by the Competition and Markets Authority, the particular characteristics of the higher education sector mean that proportionate regulation is needed to protect the interests of students, employers, and taxpayers. (p. 15)

Solution:

A new Office for Students will put competition and choice at the heart of sector regulation: it will operate a more risk-based approach so that we can focus attention where it is needed most to drive up quality. (p. 6)

The OfS will be a consumer-focused market regulator. (p. 16)
we will expect a clear demonstration of quality, and the OfS will have the powers to intervene rapidly if it has reason to believe that quality in any institution is failing. This will ensure that we maintain a high and rigorous bar for entry into the system and for providers where there is cause of concern, whilst significantly reducing the burden of inspection on those providers, whatever their historical status, where we are confident that they are performing well. (p. 33)

In effect:

Regulation of the sector will move to a new government department, the Office for Students (OfS). In effect, this now means that HE is regulated primarily by the government, subject to the ideological objectives of the mechanics of marketisation. The OfS is not a regulator of higher education but of the HE *market*. The commitment to market economy principles are highlighted further through association with the Competitions and Markets Authority (CMA).

'Quality' is seen to be an important feature of the rhetoric (*our primary goal is to raise the overall level of quality* p. 10) with the OfS holding powers to intervene if the 'high and rigorous bar for entry' is not met or maintained. However, this appears to be misleading when correlated with the CMA's own attitude towards 'quality' in a competitive market.

Within 'An effective regulatory framework for higher education: policy paper' (CMA, 2015 p. 5) the CMA suggest that a reformed regulatory framework should 'Regulate for a baseline of quality' and that new providers must meet this 'baseline level of quality' but, critically, that this 'baseline level of quality is kept to a minimum to promote competition'.

The rationale given for requirement of reformed regulation, in the form of the OfS, is 'as recognised by the CMA' but with the OfS's commitment for high standards and quality contrary to CMA's own recognitions! A commitment that quality should be 'kept to a minimum to promote competition' is damning and reveals that the OfS's role is, indeed, to regulate quality but, in effect, low quality. Low thresholds for quality will enable new providers to enter the market place, as intended, able to offer cheaper courses of lower quality, suppressing quality across the sector. How 'low quality' 'protects students' is unclear. The lowering of minimum quality standards, designed to encourage new providers to compete in the market is in direct opposition to the seemingly benevolent aims of the TEF, to raise quality. The neoliberal, market-led, ideology which provides the explanatory framework for the TEF requires the expansion of competitive markets and differential pricing of products which, naturally, leads to lower quality, lower cost providers.

THE RANGE OF POSSIBLE SOLUTIONS (ARENA 3)

It is clear that the TEF, and associated policy ensemble, sought to marketise higher education at the expense of quality. However, how did this come to be an accepted solution to the perceived problems facing the sector?

> *for any way of thought to become dominant, a conceptual apparatus has to be advanced that appeals to our intuitions and instincts, to our values and our desires, as well as to the possibilities inherent in the social world we inhabit. If*

> *successful, this conceptual apparatus becomes so embedded in common sense as to be taken for granted and not open to question.* (Harvey, 2005, p. 5)

It has already been noted that Neoliberalism is the dominant contemporary ideology. Harvey identifies that an aspect of 'domination' is in the limiting of possibilities for societal change. Scheurich concurs; the grid of social regularities 'constitute the range of acceptable policy solutions' (Scheurich, 1994, p. 303). From this perspective, the TEF was not necessarily the *best* solution for society but that most closely aligned to the dominant *vision* of societal order. 'Changes in society have created a context conducive for the ranking of university teaching' (Gunn, 2018, p. 132), as found within the TEF.

'Policy archaeology suggests that social regularities are "productive" and "reproductive" in the sense that the regularities constitute what is socially visible or credible' (Scheurich, 1994, p. 302). Only what is 'visible' can been identified as a problem and, through ideological restriction of visibility, what can be viewed as a solution is also both limited and constitutive of ideology. In this sense, the dominant ideological codes not only produce the visibility of problems, that which come into view as being problematic, but also reproduce, and reinforce the dominant ideology itself. Certain solutions become 'commonsensical' through strict adherence with the grid of regularities, rendering alternative solutions invisible, unacceptable or insane. As Fairclough concurs, discourse is a socially shaped and socially shaping action, contextualised by the norms of historical and social situations (Fairclough, 1993).

Scheurich suggests that social agents are not 'self-consciously aware of the social regularities shaping their subjectivities' (Scheurich, 1994, p. 303), linking this policy methodology to stated origins of Foucauldian thought. Foucault (1973) presents the concept of the 'already encoded eye' (xxi), things that belong 'to a certain unspoken order' (xx). Things which one does not need to speak OF due to them being WITHIN all that is spoken. Ideology can be defined as a process of encoding, 'as a body of meaning and values encoding certain interests relevant to social power ... that are unifying, action-orientated, rationalizing, legitimating, universalising, and naturalizing' which promote forth 'a system of strategies and tactics that lead to the commonplace acceptance of a particular system of beliefs' (Saunders, 2015, p. 402).

Only policy problems/solutions that appear within the range of sight of this encoded eye are recognisable. The grid of regularities act as 'preconceptual glasses or frames through which human actions and categories, including social problems and policy solutions, become socially defined' (Scheurich, 1994, p. 306). The 'lens' of neoliberalism is clearly required when viewing the policy schematics of contemporary governmentality and in developing an understanding of the impacts upon and within HE (Caanan, 2013).

Invisible alternatives 'never appear within dominant social discourses because they are incongruent with the dominant social order' (Scheurich, 1994, p. 306) this is because 'the social order would be deligitimized if it was readily apparent that inequalities, for instance, were merely historical social constructions' (Scheurich, 1994, p. 306). Social agents become encoded through ideological domination and, subsequently, encode through commonsensical discourse and action in alignment with the grid of regularities; a seemingly unstoppable process of continual neoliberalisation. In this sense higher education, through policies such as the TEF, is encoded by, with and reproductive of neoliberal ideology, producing citizens with the 'attitudes' needed to contribute to the national and international market places, complicit through socially regulated symbolic violations (Bourdieu, 1984). As Margaret Thatcher, the great neoliberalist, famously said, 'There is no alternative', or more accurately, there BECOMES no alternative as hegemonic logic limits the view of what can be possible in the future.

Neoliberalisation as Industrialisation

Despite the concerns raised by the sector through the TEF's inception and the political intention to effectively lower quality and standards, the UK Higher Education sector has adopted the TEF and its 'Olympian' medal standards. As institutions continue to feature their TEF credentials prominently on websites and marketing materials, reforming learning environments and pedagogy to more 'successfully' achieve outcomes dictated by specific metrics valued by the TEF, the neoliberalising potential of the policy has become a reality. The marketisation of higher education has been complicitly enacted by this sector once widely critical of the foundational principles and assumptions presented. Institutions have become reconfigured as reproductive engines of the encoded, visible potential of hegemonic rationality. 'Adapting' for survival within hegemony (Freire, 1974) rather than risky rejection.

'Neoliberalism has a definite view of education, understanding it as human capital formation. It is the business of forming the skills and attitudes needed by a productive workforce ... producing an ever-growing mass of profits for the market economy' (Connell, 2013, p. 104). Higher education becomes industrialised, and industrial, as alternative forms of value are modified to view primarily only the economic outcomes of graduate activity, 'employability' and earning power as measures of quality. As marketisation requires differential pricing, the debt accrued (and associated precarity) by graduates must be offset by tax receipts. As neoliberal logic constructs educational institutions as the factories where educational products are consumed by customers towards common-sense investment towards profitable futures, students become re-cast as units of economic capital potential; more akin to raw-materials cast into 'goods' (e.g. viable economic actors) through institutional mechanisms (i.e. 'excellent' teaching) than 'citizens' motivated and incentivised to imagine a wider range of social values.

Those 'inefficient' factories of the 'knowledge economy', those which are unsuccessful in outputting graduate's with profitable capital quantities, are duly awarded lower resources and positions on the competitive market platforms which seek to compare institutions. To marketise, neoliberalise and industrialise is to create systems of competition which result in hierarchical ordering against specific conceptions of only economic value. Our culture validates these specific units of value which retro-actively inform the policies and courses of actions which create the systems of worth. The connection between neoliberalism, metric based performance measures and the industrialisation of higher education can be clearly viewed through policy analysis of problems, solutions and adaptive behaviour by both institutions in a broad sense and the 'cogs in the machine' of HE's primary protagonists (students, teachers and administrators). The adoption of these types of performance measures represents severe threat for artistic subjects prophesised within parallel policy machinations playing out within UK education.

SUBJECT TEF, THE EBACC AND THE DEMISE
OF MUSIC EDUCATION

As the TEF secures its rational adoption, the next stage in the policy narrative is the subject-level or subject-specific TEF (OfS, 2020). It is unclear at the time of writing what this may involve or how, or when, findings from the subject-level TEF pilot may be implemented but there is already evidence of differential, negative, treatment of artistic subjects (e.g. those who typically do not produce economically profitable graduates). No more directly is this seen than the recent funding cut to arts courses in England rationalised as reprioritising 'taxpayers' money towards subjects that support the NHS, science, technology and engineering, and the specific needs of the labour market' (Weale, 2021, no page number). What is clear is that where subject hierarchies have been drawn, through this 'objective' lens of graduate outcomes, music education has been negatively impacted with catastrophic effect. The English Baccalaureate (EBacc) is a prime example of this.

The EBacc is a suite of subjects schools and students are encouraged to select with the government's aspiration that 90% of schools will be offering the EBacc by 2021. The rationale for the EBacc and adoption by schools is to provide the fullest range of employment options. Once again, the link between educational policy and employment outcomes are central here. A leaflet provided by the Department for Education to parents clearly highlights the primacy of employability in subject selection but also in progression towards higher education: 'While your child may not have decided on their future career path yet, choosing the EBacc at GCSE gives them access to a full range of employment options when they leave secondary school and the broad knowledge that employers are looking for. If they are thinking of going to university, the EBacc is also recommended by Britain's most prestigious universities' (DfE, 2018a, no page number).

The omission of music and other artistic subjects from the EBacc has resulted in schools turning away from the offer of Music; the hierarchising of subjects within the policy has successfully impacted upon school leader's, student's and parent's behaviours in a strikingly effective and targeted manner. An All-Party Parliamentary group report on the state of Music Education concluded that 'Government policy, particularly around accountability measures like the English Baccalaureate (EBacc), has significantly negatively impacted on music education in schools in England … causing untold damage to music and many other creative subjects in school' (ISM, 2019, pp. 2–3). This damaging marginalisation has resulted in decreased curriculum time allocation rationalised through the subject hierarchy the EBacc 'confirms' through the logic of market-based neoliberalism. Like the internalisation of the TEF by HE leaders, this logic has been adopted by a school's music sector adapting for survival, justifying the value of music as a proxy for knock-on gains in those most 'valuable' subjects of mathematics and English.

The EBacc evidences the fatal damage neoliberal 'subject-specific' policy making has wrought on music education. The EBacc has effectively weakened the pipeline of prospective students which may have considered study within higher education, the sector which is likely to soon face its own subjection to hierarchising rationality through the subject-level TEF. As Music in HE education likely becomes weakened through both negations in 'value' through adoption of TEF and fewer 'customers' into the market due to marginalisation in school, music education in HE will certainly suffer, becoming only the preserve of the elite. Rather than rejection of the EBacc, mirroring HE's own weak adaptation and complicity in adoption of the TEF, there are calls for music to be included as an EBacc subject (Underhill, 2021), further echoing the sense that alternatives to neoliberal logic are impossible, only complicity to the system is possible for survival.

As the incurable link between comparable notions of 'value' as applied across subject hierarchies, true to the confirmatory and confirming logic of neoliberalism, continue to infuse political discourse, a clear warning sounds that future evolution of the TEF is unlikely to benefit those subjects whose value lies outside of graduate earning data. Students are implicated within this rhetoric, presenting their supposed problems as basis for future policy solutions by education ministers. Neoliberal logic is invoked by higher education ministers on behalf of students to justify this neoliberal, 'value for money' rationale. '(S)tudents are far more aware of the bottom line. They want to make sure their chosen course represents good value for money, both in terms of the quality of education it provides and the future earnings it is likely to secure them' (Donelan, 2020 no page number). Student's 'problems' are aligned with those of the tax payer in relation to 'underperforming degrees' (as if the courses themselves are underperforming and therefore ripe for marginalisation); 'The clutch of underperforming degrees is a problem for students—it is likely they include many of the courses whose students feel they are not getting value for money. … They are also a problem for the taxpayer, since courses where students tend not to earn graduate salaries after graduation account for a disproportionate share of the costs to the public purse' (DfE, 2018b, no page number). The Department for Education frames these policy problems and solutions as benevolent instruments of meritocratic sensibility, consistently linking 'quality' and 'value' to the market place of jobs, economic capital and industrial outcomes. 'I also want to be clear that we will look forensically at courses to ensure they are high quality, and lead to good graduate outcomes' (DfE, 2021, no page number). 'We must never forget that the purpose of education is to give people the skills they need to get a good and meaningful job' (DfE, 2020, no page number). If we are to 'never forget' neoliberal governmentality, new futures become unimaginable, confirming hegemonic complicity to an industrialised system of cultural decay.

Conclusion

Through use of Scheurich's Policy Archaeology, it is evident that the TEF is encoded with, and reinforces, the dominant grid of social regularities. The clear relationship between the policy's 'market led' principles aligns with wider neoliberal ideology, achieving a 'common-sensical' tone within the context of existing possibilities of 'visible' action. The wider policy ensemble act as technologies of power and weapons of symbolic violence, as discourse around the nature of HE normalises, justifies and legitimises pursuit of individualistic, purely economic, outcomes at the expense of a wider societal good. The TEF seeks to 'value what is measurable rather than measuring what is valuable' (Klemencic & Ashwin, 2015, p. 8).

The University reflects the society it is within, is an 'expression of the age' (Flexner, 1930). Through this continual reflection it eventually becomes crystallised in its own, new, image; echoing, reinforcing and legitimising the initial, societal image it reflects. 'The University' is from society, of society and also TO society and constructs society as much as it is constructed by society. 'The primary function of these social constructions is to provide a definition of correct, productive behaviour to citizens who are already acting in concert with the social order' (Scheurich, 1994, p. 312). The social regularities which present policy problems and solutions become self-fulfilling when guided towards limiting potential for change in the future. Hegemony resides within this grid of social regularities, or perhaps IS the grid of regularities.

There are now plentiful examples of how neoliberal, industrialising policy negatively impacts upon subjects not conforming to the logic of economic output. To adapt to this system may facilitate temporary survival but, ultimately, complicity confirms this ideological rationale, creating conditions for future narrowing of a window of agency. As Neary provokes (Neary, 2016), seeking alternatives to neoliberalisation should become central to stakeholders across the HE sector but with the neoliberal project seeking to dis-power both academics, through precarious work conditions, and students/graduates, encoded and saddled by debt, there are many challenges. Continual reflective questioning by all HE stakeholders, especially within artistic and musical arenas must take place. How do we exercise our agency and how does this reinforce or subvert dominant ideology? Are our intentions aligned with our actions and what powers restrict these? To what extent do we have the opportunity to make change through exercise of our agency or modes of cultural capital? Who or what are we teaching for and how does this manifest within curriculum and pedagogy? How free are we to make change and why is this the case? A mainstream existence of music education in higher education depends on a critical rejection of neoliberal logic across all stages of the education system; to only adapt is to self-destruct.

REFERENCES

Ainley, P. (2004). The new 'market-state' and education. *Journal of Education Policy, 19*(4), 497–515.

Ashwin, P. W. H. (2017). What is the teaching excellence framework in the United Kingdom, and will it work? *International Higher Education, 88*, 10.

Askehave, I. (2007). The impact of marketisation on higher education genres – the international student prospectus as a case in point. *Discourse Studies, 9*(6), 723–742.

Bailey, S. (2017). From invisibility to visibility: A policy archaeology of the introduction of anti-transphobic and anti-homophobic bullying guidelines into the Irish primary education system. *Irish Education Studies, 36*(1), 25–42.

Barkas, L. A., Scott, J. M., Poppitt, N. J. & Smith, P. J. (2017). Tinker, tailor, policy-maker: Can the UK government's teaching excellence framework deliver its objectives? *Journal of further and higher education*, https://www.tandfonline.com/doi/full/10.1080/0309877X.2017.1408789. Accessed 7th Jan 2022.

Bhopal, K. (2018). *White privilege: The myth of a post-racial society*. Policy Press.

Bourdieu, P. (1984). *Distinction: A social critique of the judgement of taste.* Routledge & Kegan Paul.

Business Dictionary (2018). Market definition. http://www.businessdictionary.com/definition/market.html. Accessed 25th September 2018.

Canaan, J. E. (2013). Resisting the English Neoliberalising university: What critical pedagogy can offer. *The Journal of Critical Education Policy Studies, 11*(2), 16–56.

Competition & Markets Authority (2015). An effective regulatory framework for higher education: A policy paper. https://assets.publishing.service.gov.uk/media/550bf3c740f0b61404000001/Policy_paper_on_higher_education.pdf. Accessed 7th Jan 2022.

Connell, R. (2013). The neoliberal cascade and education: An essay on the market agenda and its consequences. *Critical Studies in Education, 54*(2), 99–112.

Cruickshank, J. (2016). Putting business at the heart of higher education: On neoliberal interventionism and audit culture in UK Universities. *Open Library Of Humanities, 2*(1), 1–33.

Department for Business, Innovation and Skills. (2015). Fulfilling our Potential: Teaching Excellence, Social Mobility and Student Choice [online] https://www.timeshighereducation.com/sites/default/files/breaking_news_files/green_paper.pdf. Accessed 7th Jan 2022.

Department for Business, Innovation and Skills. (2016a). Summary of Consultation Responses – Fulfilling our Potential: Teaching Excellence, Social Mobility and Student Choice. https://assets.publishing.service.gov.uk/government/uploads/system/uploads/attachment_data/file/523420/bis-16-261-he-green-paper-fulfilling-our-potential-summary-of-responses.pdf. Accessed 7th Jan 2022.

Department for Business, Innovation and Skills. (2016b). Success as a Knowledge Economy: Teaching Excellence, Social Mobility and Student Choice. https://www.gov.uk/government/publications/higher-education-success-as-a-knowledge-economy-white-paper. Accessed 7th Jan 2022.

Department for Education (2016). Teaching Excellence Framework: analysis of highly skilled employment outcomes. https://www.gov.uk/government/publications/teaching-excellence-framework-highly-skilled-employment-outcomes. Accessed 7th January 2022.

Department for Education (2018a). Help Your Child Make the Best GSCE Choices. https://assets.publishing.service.gov.uk/government/uploads/system/uploads/attachment_data/file/761031/DfE_EBacc_Leaflet.pdf. Accessed 7th January 2022.

Department for Education. (2018b). Delivering value for money in the age of the student. https://www.gov.uk/government/speeches/delivering-value-for-money-in-the-age-of-the-student. Accessed 7th January 2022.

J. HUXTABLE

Department for Education. (2020). Education Secretary FE speech with Social Market Foundation. https://www.gov.uk/government/speeches/education-secretary-fe-speech-with-social-market-foundation?utm_source=3d8b2e7a-4bc0-47b2-822c-1fc489d8608e&utm_medium=email&utm_campaign=govuk-notifications&utm_content=immediate. Accessed 7th January 2022.

Department for Education. (2021). Higher and Further Education Minister speech at Times Higher Education event. https://www.gov.uk/government/speeches/higher-and-further-education-minister-speech-at-times-higher-education-event. Accessed 7th January 2022.

Donelan, M. (2020). Universities minister announces crackdown on 'low quality' courses. https://www.telegraph.co.uk/news/2020/02/29/universities-minister-announces-crackdown-low-quality-courses/. Accessed 7th January 2022.

Fairclough, N. (1993). Critical discourse analysis and the marketisation of public discourse: The universities. *Discourse and Society, 4*(2), 133–168.

Flexner. (1930). *Universities American English German.* Oxford University Press.

Foucault, M. (1973). *The order of things: And archaeology of the human sciences.* Vintage Books.

Freedman, D. (2011). The Assault on Universities: An Introduction to Education Reform and Resistance. http://www.counterfire.org/the-assault-on-universities/15113-the-assault-on-universities-an-introduction-to-education-reform-and-resistance. Accessed 7th January 2022.

Freire. (1972). *Pedagogy of the oppressed.* Herder and Herder.

Freire. (1974). Freire: Education for critical consciousness.

Gale, T. (2001). Critical policy sociology: Historiography, archaeology and genealogy as methods of policy analysis. *Journal of Education Policy, 16*(5), 379–393.

Gillard, J. W. (2018). An initial analysis and reflection of the metrics used in the teaching excellence framework in the UK. *Perspectives: Policy and Practice in Higher Education, 22*(2), 49–57.

Giroux, H. (2014). *Neoliberalism's war on higher education.* Haymarket Books.

Gunn, A. (2018). Metrics and methodologies for measuring teaching quality in higher education: Developing the teaching excellence framework (TEF). *Educational Review, 70*(2), 129–148.

Harvey, D. (2005). *A brief history of neoliberalism.* Oxford University Press.

Heaney, C., & Mackenzie, H. (2017). The teaching excellence framework: Perpetual pedagogical control in postwelfare capitalism. *Compass: Journal of Learning and Teaching., 10*, 2.

Higher Education Research Act. (2017). http://www.legislation.gov.uk/ukpga/2017/29/contents/enacted. Accessed 7th January 2022.

Important India (2016). Market Economy: Meaning, Features, Advantages and Disadvantages. https://www.importantindia.com/23753/market-economy/. Accessed 7th Jan 2022.

Institute for Fiscal Studies (IFS). (2011). Higher Education funding in England: past, present and options for the future. https://ifs.org.uk/sites/default/files/output_url_files/BN211.pdf. Accessed 7th January 2022.

ISM. (2019). Music Education: State of the Nation – Report by the All-Party Parliamentary Group for Music Education, the Incorporated Society of Musicians and the University of Sussex. https://www.ism.org/images/images/FINAL-State-of-the-Nation-Music-Education-for-email-or-web-2.pdf. Accessed 7th Jan 2022.

Klemencic, M., & Ashwin, P. (2015). *New directions for teaching, learning, and student engagement in the.* European Higher Education Area. http://scholar.harvard.edu/files/manja_klemencic/files/klemencic_and_ashwin_2015_new_directions_for_teaching_and_learning_in_europe.pdf. Accessed: 27th Sept 2018

Lemke, T. (2001). 'The birth of bio-politics': Michel Foucault's lecture at the Collège de France on neoliberal governmentality. *Economy and Society, 30*(2), 190–207.

Lucas, C. (2018). 'Use of Kano modelling to analyse module surveys and prioritise improvement measures'. In advance HE surveys conference 2018, Leeds, 9th may 2018. https://www.heacademy.ac.uk/knowledge-hub/advance-he-surveys-conference-2018-use-kano-modelling-claire-lucas. Accessed 7th Jan 2022.

Mautner. (2005). The entrepreneurial university: A discursive profile of a higher education buzzword. *Critical Discourse Studies, 2*(2), 95–120.

Neary, M. (2016). Teaching excellence framework: A critical response and an alternative future. *Journal of Contemporary European Research, 12*(3), 690–695.

OfS. (2020). Future of the TEF. https://www.officeforstudents.org.uk/advice-and-guidance/teaching/future-of-the-tef/. Accessed 7th Jan 2022.

Olssen, M., & Peters, M. A. (2005). Neoliberalism, higher education and the knowledge economy: From the free market to knowledge capitalism. *Journal of Education Policy, 20*(3), 313–345.

Race, P. (2017). The teaching excellence framework (TEF): Yet more competition – And on the wrong things! *Compass: Journal of Learning and Teaching., 10*(2).

Radice, H. (2013). How we got here: UK higher education under neoliberalism. *ACME., 12*(3), 407–418.

Saunders, D. B. (2015). Resisting excellence: Challenging neoliberal ideology in postsecondary education. *The Journal of Critical Education Policy Studies, 13*(2), 391–413.

Scheurich, J. J. (1994). Policy archaeology: A new policy studies methodology. *Journal of Education Policy, 9*(4), 297–316.

The Balance. (2018). Market Economy, Its Characteristics, Pros, and Cons, with Examples. https://www.thebalance.com/market-economy-characteristics-examples-pros-cons-3305586. Accessed 7th Jan 2022.

Underhill, J. (2021). Education Select Committee Renews Call For Music To Be Included in the EBACC. https://www.classical-music.uk/news/article/education-select-committee-renews-call-for-music-to-be-included-in-the-ebacc-1. Accessed 7th Jan 2022.

Universities UK. (2017). Review of the Teaching Excellence Framework Year 2. https://issuu.com/universitiesuk/docs/review-of-the-teaching-excellence-f. Accessed 1st Mar 2022.

Walton, G. (2010). The problem trap: Implications of policy archaeology methodology for anti-bullying policies. *Journal of Education Policy, 25*(2), 135–150.

Weale, S. (2021). Funding cuts to go ahead for university arts courses in England despite opposition. https://www.theguardian.com/education/2021/jul/20/funding-cuts-to-go-ahead-for-university-arts-courses-in-england-despite-opposition. Accessed 7th Jan 2022.

Wilby, P. (2013). Margaret Thatcher's education legacy is still with us – driven on by Gove. https://www.theguardian.com/education/2013/apr/15/margaret-thatcher-education-legacy-gove. Accessed 7th Jan 2022.

Wood, M., & Su, F. (2017). What makes an excellent lecturer? Academics' perspectives on the discourse of 'teaching excellence' in higher education. *Teaching in Higher Education, 22*(4), 451–466.

Conclusion

Samantha Broadhead

Abstract The conclusion will recap briefly on some of the points made by the chapter writers and attempt to draw together some important threads that have arisen from their work. It will revisit some of the tensions between arts education and industry and how educators have responded creatively to the complex contexts in which they operate. Three orientations of industrialisation and arts education can be seen in relation to the chapters of this book. These are: educating students to meet the needs of industry; the influence of industrialisation on arts educational philosophy and art practices and the measurement, standardisation and instrumentalism of educational policies.

Keywords Art • Higher education • Industry • Creative Industries • Instrumentalism • Education

S. Broadhead (✉)
Leeds Arts University, Leeds, UK
e-mail: sam.broadhead@leeds-art.ac.uk

151

Overview

The conclusion will recap briefly on some of the points made by the chapter writers and attempt to draw together some important threads that have arisen from their work. It will revisit some of the tensions between arts education and industry and how educators have responded creatively to the complex contexts in which they operate. Three orientations of industrialisation and arts education can be seen in relation to the chapters of this book. These are:

- Educating students to meet the needs of industry;
- The influence of industrialisation on arts educational philosophy and art practices;
- The measurement, standardisation and instrumentalism of educational policies.

Educating Students to Meet the Needs of Industry

The first art and design schools in the UK aspired to educate their students for local industries in order to benefit the quality of goods and services through raising the quality of creativity and design (Romans, 2005; Cooksey, 2006). This aim broadly continued throughout the next two centuries. Broadhead's historical study into post-war design education reveals that art schools, such as the Royal College of Art saw that working in industry was an important part of a creative person's education. Broadhead considers the experience of a student undertaking work placement in the 1950s which was responsive to the needs of a jewellery manufacturer that was local to the student's home.

Broadhead's case study based on the experiences of jewellery maker Ann O'Donnell when she was a student on a work placement at Charles Horner Ltd illuminates the ways in which design education engaged with industry during the post-war era. The innovation that occurred during the 1950s that happened in design-led jewellery has been attributed to the influence of the arts schools (Reinhold, 2008). Phillips (1996) noted that many design graduates opened up small businesses and commercial galleries. However, to what extent the art school curriculum prepared their students for working in larger scale manufacturing companies is uncertain.

O'Donnell's story suggested that there was a contrast in cultures between the College and her work placement. The firm did not make use of her design creativity to enhance their product line, but did draw upon her technical skills to make the factory line more efficient. O'Donnell was able to learn a lot about how to organise the work place and manage resources, skills and knowledge that did not seem to be a significant part of her art school training. After a year the work placement ended and O'Donnell decided that working in industry was not for her.

Ironically, O'Donnell spent her subsequent teaching career training workers from the local Leeds Jewellery trade. However, this was through teaching part-time, day-release and evening classes. This mode of delivery suited the needs of her students as it was flexible and responsive, but perhaps was not perceived by the art school management as being as significant as those teaching on full-time courses (Kropf, 2001; Moen & Roehling, 2005; Webber & Williams, 2008).

One theme that reoccurs in O'Donnell's account is a tension between educating arts students to be experimental, where drawing and making were part of the design process, and the employment of her craft skills within an industrial context. Unlike the vision of Gropius (1965) where the Bauhaus and its alumni contributed towards industry in clearly defined ways, there seems to be an ambiguity in how the education-industry relationship would work practically in O'Donnell's case.

Smith's reflective account of educating for the animation industry brings some of the issues introduced in Broadhead's historical case study into a contemporary context. Smith's critique focuses on educating for the creative industries (these can be local, national or global organisations). He frames the debate as the 'animation educator's dilemma' where they are cognizant that the creative industries require graduates to have a high level of training and technical understanding, but also believe in students receiving a well-rounded education. Smith points out that skills acquisition cannot be the sole responsibility of higher education and can only be fully realised through an ongoing dialogue with industry representatives such as the UK Animation Alliance (2019). At the same time Smith argues there should be an acknowledgement of the broader remit of a university education that goes beyond training, such as the development of creativity and innovation, critical thinking and social responsibility.

An education purely based on skills development would be risky and not necessarily beneficial for either students or employers. This is because of the breadth of possible technologies and platforms used by various animation companies, and also the fast rate of technical and digital innovation which could make some specific skills quickly redundant. How do educators decide which set of skills would have most longevity and relevance without a close dialogical relationship with the animation industry?

The Influence of Industrialisation on Arts Educational Philosophy and Art Practices

Tobias-Green and Snare consider the impact industrialisation has had on the teaching of their subjects, whilst recognising other, competing drivers that higher education must attend to. They both take a personal perspective rooted in their experiences of designing and delivering contemporary arts curricula.

Coming from a creative writing background Tobias-Green draws upon her imagination to visualise her discipline as being at the eye of the storm around which notions of industry, technology and revolution whirl and crash into one another. Snare conceptualises herself as an educator operating at the intersection between the industrial growth society, the Earth and arts education. Both writers conceptualise their teaching practice as a focal point where contradictions are experienced and managed through a consideration of the personal values each practitioner holds.

Snare reveals that as a practitioner she needs to constantly navigate through the discipline of fashion branding that she teaches, the ecological values she hopes to embody and the understanding that industrial growth has damaged the Earth (Priestley et al., 2015). At the same time, she feels a responsibility towards her students who study her subject so they can, in the future, work in the fashion industry. Snare presents her reflective account as an emotional journey citing frustration, upset, pride, fear, joy, embarrassment and disgust, springing from her engagement with the tensions she experiences throughout her teaching practice. What is evident from Snare's account is that she does not polarise industry, or educating people for careers in industry as inherently bad in relation to teaching for ecological awareness as virtuous. Rather, they are both necessities of her role and need to be attended to in a way that is transformative for both her students and the future of the Earth.

Tobias-Green, in a similar way to Snare's refusal of polarisation, aims to avoid thinking in binary oppositions between analogue and digital forms of creative arts writing. Her values are related to inclusive and democratising pedagogies that open up writing opportunities for all (Tobias-Green, 2021). The role that technological processes, associated with different historical and contemporary forms of industrial revolution, play are not vilified by Tobias-Green. Rather she sees them as potentially enabling different writers, different voices to engage with her subject.

At the same time, Tobias-Green argues that regardless of whether or not writing is technologised, teachers should strive to remain student-centred and ethical so that arts education does not become depersonalised. Her line of reasoning culminates in the suggestion that educators should be watchful of the consequences of the methods they employ, whether that is digital, analogue or a hybrid of both.

MEASUREMENT, STANDARDISATION AND INSTRUMENTALISM IN EDUCATIONAL POLICIES

Industrial processes such as the division of labour, mechanisation, rationalism and instrumentalism have influenced educational policies and institutional structures that in turn have had an impact on arts education. Esmond (addressing technical education) and Huxtable (in relation to the Teaching Excellence Framework [TEF] in higher education) consider the ways that current educational policies that focus on meeting instrumental objectives continue to marginalise the arts, constructing them as of 'low value'.

Technical education seeks to address social inequalities by leading its students into more direct employment rather than undertaking (in this case) an arts degree. Students, particularly those who are deemed 'low-achieving', are encouraged to increase their employability by accumulating 'marketable skills' (Young, 2006; Atkins, 2009). At the same time Esmond points out that policy has led to the creative and design route being placed on the margins of technical education reforms. Esmond contends that arts subjects do not easily fit with models of technical education that place students in work contexts. Also, the types of careers that this route offers may expose them to the stratified cultural industries where only those with social and cultural capitals can access desirable, creative roles with good working conditions (Reay et al., 2003). He warns that the arts are becoming separated from the technical education curriculum and arts education would then only be available to those privileged enough to undertake an arts subject in higher education.

Esmond argues that the working lives of people and how they learn about the world of work needs to be radically reconsidered. Recognising the ways in which arts and culture organise their work placements, apprenticeships and internships could open up new ways of thinking for technical and work-based education in general.

Huxtable's analysis of the TEF, through the lens of Scheurich's (1994) policy archaeology, exposes its market-led principles that align with a wider neoliberal ideology. Furthermore, he argues that, in conjunction with wider policy drives, music education is devalued because the TEF justifies and legitimises pursuit of individualistic, purely economic, outcomes at the expense of a wider societal good.

The means of using the TEF to make judgements about the quality of teaching is applied in the same to all subject areas and in that sense in standardised, allowing no variation in what is measured. The arts for example, may provide valuable contributions to society, in terms cultural life, social cohesion, health and well-being rather than purely economic ones. That is not to say that the arts do not have economic benefit, but it may take an arts graduate longer to get a highly paid position and they may not be ultimately motivated by financial reward (Broadhead, 2020).

Huxtable goes on to claim that there are many examples of how neoliberal, industrialising policies negatively impact upon creative subjects not conforming to the logic of economic output. He proposes that higher education stakeholders (students, academics, senior management, representatives of the creative industries) should continue to challenge the dominant discourses within the TEF, especially those working in artistic and musical subject areas. This should begin by asking fundamental questions about who or what are we teaching for and how this is manifested within arts curriculum and pedagogy? Huxtable ends his chapter by suggesting that for music return to mainstream higher education there needs to be a rejection of instrumental policies and structures such as the TEF.

Final Reflections

Many of the chapters argue for a wider role for arts education beyond the notion that it merely services the needs of industry. Art schools and universities need to address issues other than employability such as widening participation (Broadhead, 2022), sustainable practice (Owens, 2017; Zamora-Polo et al., 2019) and supporting the civic society (Goddard & Kempton, 2016). Some of these other imperatives potentially conflict with the need to educate graduates for manufacturing or the creative industries. For example, there are moral aspects of preparing students for working in industries that are not inclusive and where some of the less advantaged trainees may be treated unfairly. Banks (2017) has pointed out the unfair working conditions that can occur in the cultural industries; how can educational institutions address this wider societal problem? Snare has also described the tensions arts lecturers feel when educating students for the fashion industry while ensuring they have ecologically sensitive practices.

Another theme which is repeated periodically throughout the book is the ambiguous relationships between skill, craft, design and industry that have continued since public design education was instigated in the nineteenth century (Frayling, 1987). Some employers and educational policy writers do not recognise how creativity and technical ability need to be intertwined to be most effective, innovative and sustainable. Related to this point is that training people in a range of skills can only be beneficial in the short term as processes and technologies continually evolve. Any lack of dialogue between educators and industry representatives when planning curricula and work-based learning leads to a lack of appreciation of each stakeholder's concerns and remits.

On a practical level, how can an individual with an arts school education be transposed into an industrial or manufacturing context for the benefit of all involved? How do employers in the arts provide quality work placements when many of those arts organisations are small enterprises and cannot afford the time and resource? Also, what happens when a design brand is so large that the student/trainee does not gain an appropriate or meaningful experience working in design practice?

For positive relationships to develop, learning and work should no longer occur in sector silos, but be conceived of as part of a continuum. The needs of industry are often translated through governmental policies directed at forging education-industry links. But, more discussion is required between arts educational institutions and industry leaders about creating areas of common agreement such as the meanings, values, expectations and language around work placements and work-based curricula.

What will the future of arts education be and what role can it play in the fourth industrial revolution? Due to recent changes in the UK secondary, post-16 and higher education sectors there is an overriding concern about how the pipeline of talent (from school to further and higher education to employment) can be maintained so that the creative industries can benefit from highly creative and innovative workers (Broadhead et al., 2022). There have been concerns that the English baccalaureate certificate (EBacc) introduced in 2011 has been detrimental to the arts courses as young people (at school) are dissuaded from studying arts subjects because they are perceived as not being part of a core curriculum and as a result are devalued (Thomson et al., 2020; Bath et al., 2020; Fautley, 2019; Johnes, 2017; Neumann et al., 2016). As Esmond has discussed there is uncertainty in further education about how T-Levels will serve the creative arts as well as what the impact will be due to the loss of Business and Technology Education Council qualifications (BTECs) on the technical roles found in the creative sector. Finally, arts higher education is also facing funding cuts and possible limits to the numbers of students who can study creative subjects (Fazackerley, 2021; Weale, 2021). This culminates in a situation where the future for arts education in England in particular is precarious and the impact of this on the creative industries likely to be troubling.

Policies that seek to drive a connection between arts education and industry often do not take a wide view on the reasons why people study. The motivations of students are complex and are not solely driven by financial or career goals (Broadhead, 2020). There is value from the arts for manufacturing and the creative industries but creativity is also a critical part of living a good life such as being healthy and having well-being and contributing towards cultural, social and political life. So, any relationship that arts education has with industry should also address the lives, hopes and dreams of artists, craftspeople and designers—of people.

REFERENCES

Animation UK. (2019). We need to talk about skills: A skills analysis of the UK Animation industry. London. https://www.animationuk.org/news/animation-uk-we-need-to-talk-about-skills/ Accessed 07 March 2022

Atkins, L. (2009). *Invisible students, impossible dreams: Experiencing vocational education* (pp. 14–19). Trentham.

Banks, M. (2017). *Creative justice: Cultural industries, work and inequality.* Rowman & Littlefield.

Bath, N., Daubney, A., Mackrill, D., & Spruce, G. (2020). The declining place of music education in schools in England. *Children & Society, 34*(5), 443–457.

Broadhead, S. (2020). Mature students matter in art and design education. *Proceedings of Adult Education in Global Times,* 75–81.

Broadhead, S. (2022). Introduction. In S. Broadhead (Ed.), *Access and widening participation in arts higher education.* Springer.

Broadhead, S. Thompson, P. & Burns, H. (2022). *What are the long-term benefits of investing in art, craft & design in education for learning, culture, wellbeing and society?* Preliminary report. APPG Art, Craft and Design and NSEAD

Education https://www.nsead.org/files/197d15c23cc9301bb69acb742bd3f
dcd.pdf. Accessed 03 March 2022.

Cooksey, H. (2006). The impact of educational reform on the Wolverhampton
School of Art. https://scholar.google.co.uk/scholar?hl=en&as_sdt=0%2C5&
q=The+impact+of+educational+reform+on+the+Wolverhampton+School+of+
Art&btnG. Accessed 04 February 2022.

Fautley, M. (2019). The implications of evaluation and educational policy reforms
on English secondary school music education. *Arts Education Policy Review*,
120(3), 140–148. https://doi.org/10.1080/10632913.2018.1532369

Fazackerley, A. (2021). Ministers could limit student numbers on lower-earning
arts degrees in England. https://www.theguardian.com/education/2021/
oct/23/ministers-could-limit-student-numbers-lower-earning-art-degrees.
Accessed 25 October 2021.

Frayling, C. (1987). *The Royal College of Art: One hundred and fifty years of art
and design.* Barrie and Jenkins.

Goddard, J., & Kempton, L. (2016). The Civic University: Universities in leadership and management of place. https://eprints.ncl.ac.uk/file_store/productio
n/227721/93F7E065-1286-4171-9DC2-D6399E31D5BE.pdf. Accessed 03
March 2022.

Gropius, W. (1965). *The new architecture and the Bauhaus.* Massachusetts Institute
of Technology Press.

Kropf, M. B. (2001). Part-time work arrangements and the corporation: A
dynamic interaction. In R. Hertz & N. L. Marshall (Eds.), *Working families:
The transformation of the American home* (pp. 152–167). University of
California Press.

Moen, P., & Roehling, P. (2005). *The career mystique.* Rowman & Littlefield.

Neumann, E., Towers, E., Gewirtz, S., & Maguire, M. (2016). *A curriculum for
all? The effects of recent key stage 4 curriculum, assessment and accountability
reforms on English secondary education.* Kings College. http://downloads2.
dodsmonitoring.com/downloads/Misc_Files/KingsCollege141116.pdf.
Accessed 01 Nov 2021

Owens, T. L. (2017). Higher education in the sustainable development goals
framework. *European Journal of Education, 52*(4), 414–420.

Phillips, C. (1996). *Jewellery: From antiquity to present.* Thames and Hudson.

Priestley, M., Biesta, G., & Robinson, S. (2015). *Teacher agency: An ecological
approach.* Bloomsbury Publishing.

Reay, D., David, M., & Ball, S. (2003). *Higher education and social class.*
Routledge.

Reinhold, L. (2008). *Modern jewellery design: Past and present.* Arnoldsche art
publishers.

Romans, M. (2005). *Histories of art and design education: Collected essays.*
Intellect Books.

Scheurich, J. J. (1994). Policy archaeology: A new policy studies methodology. *Journal of Education Policy, 9*(4), 297–316.

Thomson, P., Hall, C., Earl, L., & Geppert, C. (2020). Subject choice as everyday accommodation/resistance: Why students in England (still) choose the arts. *Critical Studies in Education, 61*(5), 545–560.

Tobias-Green, K. (2021). *Stories from an art institution: The writing lives of students with dyslexia* (PhD thesis) Sheffield Hallam University. Available at: http://shura.shu.ac.uk/27368/. Accessed 03 Mar 2022.

Weale, S. (2021). Funding cuts to go ahead for university arts courses in England despite opposition. https://www.theguardian.com/education/2021/jul/20/funding-cuts-to-go-ahead-for-university-arts-courses-in-england-despite-opposition. Accessed 25 Oct 2021.

Webber, G., & Williams, C. (2008). Mothers in "good" and "bad" part-time jobs: Different problems, same results. *Gender & Society, 22*(6), 752–777.

Young, M. F. D. (2006). Reforming the further education and training curriculum: An international perspective. In M. Young & J. Gamble (Eds.), *Knowledge, curriculum and qualifications for South African further education* (pp. 46–63). HSRC Press.

Zamora-Polo, F., Sánchez-Martín, J., Corrales-Serrano, M., & Espejo-Antúnez, L. (2019). What do university students know about sustainable development goals? A realistic approach to the reception of this UN program amongst the youth population. *Sustainability, 11*(13), 3533.

GLOSSARY

Advanced-level qualifications (A-levels) A-Levels are subject-based qualifications that can lead to university, further study, training or work.

Bachelor of Arts (BA) BA is a bachelor's degree awarded for an undergraduate programme in the arts, or in some cases other disciplines.

British Film Institute (BFI) The BFI is a film and television charitable organisation which promotes and preserves film-making and television in the United Kingdom.

Business and Technology Education Council qualifications (BTECs) BTECs are vocational qualifications that are equivalent to other qualifications, such as the General Certificate of Secondary Education (GCSE) (BTEC levels 1 to 2), A-Levels (BTEC level 3) and university degrees (BTEC levels 6 to 7).

Creative Industries Council (CIC) The CIC is a forum of government, creative businesses and other creative organisations. It focuses on areas where there are barriers to growth of UK creative sectors such as access to finance, skills, export markets, regulation, intellectual property and infrastructure.

Council for National Academic Awards (CNAA) The CNAA was the national degree-awarding authority in the United Kingdom from 1965 until its dissolution on 20 April 1993.

Design and Art Technical Education Council (DATEC) DATECs were an association which created art and design technical qualifications. These qualifications later became BTEC courses.

© The Author(s), under exclusive license to Springer Nature Switzerland AG 2022
S. Broadhead (ed.), *The Industrialisation of Arts Education*,
https://doi.org/10.1007/978-3-031-05017-6

Department for Business, Innovation and Skills (BIS) BIS was the British government department responsible for business regulation and skills, as well as Higher and Further Education.

Diploma in Design from the Royal Art College (Des. R.A.C.) The Des. R.A.C. was a design qualification awarded by the Royal College of Art in the 1950s.

Department for Education (DfE) The DfE is the British government department responsible for child protection, education, apprenticeships and wider skills in England.

Diploma in Art and Design (DipAD) The DipAD was an art and design qualification that was eventually replaced by the BA and BA(hons) qualifications.

European Union (EU) The EU is a political and economic union of 27 member states that are located primarily in Europe.

FXPhd FXPhd is an organisation which delivers professional 3D and visual effects training.

General Certificate of Secondary Education (GCSE) GCSE is an academic qualification in a particular subject, taken in England, Wales and Northern Ireland.

Higher education (HE) HE—also called post-secondary education, third-level or tertiary education—is an optional final stage of formal learning that occurs after completion of secondary education.

Higher Education Funding Council for England (HEFCE) The HEFCE was a non-departmental public body in the United Kingdom, which was responsible for the distribution of funding for higher education to universities and further education colleges in England since 1992.

Her Majesty's Revenue and Customs (HMRC) The HMRC is a non-ministerial department of the UK Government responsible for the collection of taxes, the payment of some forms of state support and the administration of other regulatory regimes including the national minimum wage and the issuance of national insurance numbers.

Industrial Arts Bursaries Competitions (IABCs) The IABCs were competitions organised by the UK Industrial Art Bursaries Board. Successful candidates were awarded funding to develop art and design projects and to broaden their knowledge and experience.

International Centre for Guidance Studies (iCeGS) The iCeGS is a research centre with an expertise in career development and widening access. The Centre conducts research, provides consultancy to the career sector, offers a range of training and delivers a number of accredited learning programmes up to and including doctoral level.

Institute of Environmental Sciences (IES) The IES is a membership organisation representing the full spectrum of environmental disciplines, such as air quality, land condition, marine science and education.

Institute for Apprenticeships and Technical Education (IfATE) The IfATE is an executive non-departmental public body sponsored by the UK Department for Education.

Industrial Growth Society (IGS) IGS is a society that has as its basis a continuous growth in the output of industrial products, one where questions about whether these products are life necessities are not treated as important questions.

Leeds Arts University (LAU) LAU is a specialist art further and higher education institution, based in the city of Leeds, West Yorkshire, England, with a main campus opposite the University of Leeds.

Longitudinal Education Outcomes (LEO) LEO is a database which connects individuals' education data with their employment, benefits and earnings data to create a de-identified person-level administrative dataset.

Limited company (Ltd) A limited company is where the liability of members or subscribers of the company is limited to what they have invested (notably shares or guarantees).

Machine aesthetic Where art and design acknowledges and celebrates industrialisation, mass-production and engineering by designing using forms that could be created by mechanistic processes.

National Council for Diplomas in Art and Design (NCDAD) NCDAD was a UK statutory body responsible for awarding Diplomas in Art and Design undertaken in further education colleges. It operated from 1961 to 1974, when its responsibilities were merged into the Council for National Academic Awards.

National Diploma in Design (NDD) The NDD was an art and design qualification that was eventually replaced by the DipAD qualification.

Organisation for Economic Co-operation and Development (OECD) OECD is an intergovernmental economic organisation with 38 member countries, founded in 1961 to stimulate economic progress and world trade.

Office for Students (OfS)   The OfS is an independent regulator of higher education in England that works with higher education providers to make sure that students succeed in higher education.

Participation of Local Areas (POLAR)   POLAR are classification groups areas across the UK based on the proportion of young people who participate in higher education.

Quality Assurance Agency for Higher Education (QAA)   The QAA is the independent body that checks on standards and quality in UK higher education. It conducts quality-assessment reviews, develops reference points and guidance for providers and conducts or commissions research on relevant issues.

Royal Air Force (RAF)   The RAF is the United Kingdom's air and space force.

Royal Society of the Arts (RSA)   The RSA is a London-based organisation founded in 1754. The RSA is committed to finding practical solutions to social challenges in the arts.

Staybrite   Staybrite steel did not tarnish and was used to make costume jewellery in the mid-twentieth century because it could be moulded to look like pave diamonds or marcasite.

Science, Technology, Engineering, Arts and Mathematics (STEAM)   STEAM is a broad term that groups academic disciplines together and recognises the arts as a core subject.

Science, Technology, Engineering and Mathematics (STEM)   STEM is a broad term used to group together these academic disciplines.

Sustainable Development Goals (SDGs)   The SDGs are a collection of 17 interlinked global goals designed to be a "blueprint to achieve a better and more sustainable future for all". The SDGs were set up in 2015 by the United Nations General Assembly and are intended to be achieved by the year 2030.

T-Levels   T-Levels are technical-based qualifications in England developed in collaboration with employers and businesses so that the content meets the needs of industry and prepares students for work, further training or study.

Teaching Excellence and Student Outcomes Framework (TEF)   The TEF is a national exercise, introduced by the government in England. Its aim has been to assess excellence in teaching at higher education providers and assess how they ensure excellent outcomes for their students in terms of graduate-level employment or further study.

University of the Arts London (UAL)   UAL is a collegiate university in London, England, specialising in arts, design, fashion and the performing arts.

Vocational Education and Training (VET)   VET is a sector that ensures skills development in a wide range of occupational fields, through school-based and work-based learning.

Visual Effects (sometimes abbreviated VFX)   VFX is the process by which imagery is created or manipulated outside the context of a live-action shot in film-making and video production.

INDEX

Lightning Source UK Ltd.
Milton Keynes UK
UKHW021839160223
417113UK00002B/57